WOODBERRY FOREST:

A Venture in Faith

Woodberry Forest School Today

WOODBERRY FOREST:

A Venture in Faith

by

ELIZABETH COPELAND
NORFLEET

Published by
THE GEORGIAN PRESS, INC., NEW YORK 14, N.Y.
1955

Reprinted 1988
Woodbery Forest School
Office of External Affairs
Woodberry Forest, Virginia 22989

To John Carter Walker

Who for fifty years has been the HEADMASTER *of* WOODBERRY FOREST SCHOOL:

Who from an insignificant beginning has built the SCHOOL *into a position of preeminence;*

Who, by a rigid insistence upon high standards of scholarship, has won for the SCHOOL *the recognition of the best Colleges and Universities;*

Who, by his own unswerving adherence to the highest moral and intellectual integrity, has made a lasting impression for good upon the lives of hundreds of young men who have passed through the SCHOOL: *and*

Whose unyielding ideals of pedagogy have been a constant inspiration to us, his colleagues:

This expression of esteem has been presented by the FACULTY *of* WOODBERRY FOREST SCHOOL, *with the hope that he may enjoy many years of rest and relaxation from the arduous labors of the past half-century, and may find frequent and well-earned satisfaction in reflecting upon a life spent in the service of young men.*

A copy of the Scroll presented by the Faculty of Woodberry Forest School to Mr. Walker upon his retirement as headmaster in 1948.

JOHN CARTER WALKER
Headmaster of Woodberry Forest School
1897-1948

The Georgian Press, Inc.
175 Varick Street, New York 14, N. Y.

DESIGNED AND PRINTED BY THE GEORGIAN PRESS, INC., NEW YORK

A PREFACE

FAITH IN THEIR BOYS is what Captain and Mrs. Robert Stringfellow Walker used as the cornerstone of Woodberry Forest School. Those first six Woodberry boys and all others following after them have testified to the fact that "faith, if it hath not works, is dead, being alone".

This is the anecdotal history of the school, not its definitive history, and as such ends with the retirement of the Walker family from the active direction of the school which was created around their personalities. Here we have recorded the heritage of the new Woodberry Forest, a history now in the making.

This little story might properly be sub-titled, "The Romance of Woodberry Forest". As such, it is actually the compilation of reminiscences of many Woodberry Forest boys, chief among whom is Joseph G. Walker. Without what he naively calls his "Notes", this story could never have been written.

However, "Mr. Joe" is not the only Woodberry boy whose recollections of the past have been used as source material by the writer of this narrative. Lewis C. Williams, calling himself "An Old Alumnus", wrote a pamphlet which has been of great value. A number of other "Old Boys" have been generous indeed in offering material for use in this volume. Chief among them is A. Stuart Robertson, who gave the writer invaluable aid by compiling the financial background for the original incorporation and for the transfer of the property to the Alumni. Among others whose reminiscences have been used are Thomas B. Jackson, Edward C. Anderson, Mr. Robertson and the Walker family, as well as many devoted denizens, past and present, of Woodberry Forest. They include Arthur Latham, Mr. and Mrs. W. Leland Lord, Miss Constance Johnson, Mrs. Russell Bargamin and Mr. and Mrs. R. W. D. Taylor.

The writer is further indebted to other alumni and friends of the school for their eager and generous assistance in reading and correcting the manuscript. Bosley Crowther, motion picture editor of The *New York Times,* and Coleman C. Walker, Chairman of the Board of Trustees of Woodberry Forest School, stand first among these, although valuable aid in this field was rendered also by James W. Cobbs, Leon Dure, Henry W. Mattfield and Mr. Latham. Mr. Lord's moral support, indefatigable assistance in selecting material and pictures, and wholehearted approbation have been vital elements in the production of this work.

One special word of gratitude for furnishing critical assistance over a period of many years must be said of Virginia Hulvey Snead. Without her always exact and ever understanding interpretation of every factor in the life and spirit of the School, the writer would have been as uneducated in the background for this work as she would have been unwilling to attempt it without the enthusiastic encouragement of Coleman Walker.

One final gesture of gratitude must be made to the friend of Woodberry Forest who has, anonymously, made this little book a gift to the School.

ELIZABETH COPELAND NORFLEET

Woodberry Forest, Virginia
March 1955

Contents

Chapter I

THE BIRTH OF A DREAM

ROBERT STRINGFELLOW WALKER was a man who never asked questions of fate. And as the good soldier he became, he never questioned the order of his commanding officer whoever he chanced to be – his teacher, his colonel, his father or his God.

When the Civil War started, Bob Walker was a student at Randolph-Macon College at Boydton, Virginia. He had gone there, his son Joe tells us, with his axe in his trunk and his pocketknife in his trousers. Apparently with these and his talent for real leadership, to which all of his sons continually refer, he kept warm, attended to his own business and made many friends, as indicated, among other things, by his membership in Delta Psi, the fraternity often known as St. Anthony.

Even so, he did not join his schoolmates when, in chauvinistic zeal, they rushed off to enlist upon Virginia's secession from the Union. He went home to "Rosni" in Madison County, where he had been born in 1840 to John Scott Walker and Susan Herndon Stringfellow Walker. His father was a strong believer in the strength of the Union, and Bob Walker decided to consult the paternal wishes before making his own decision.

At home he found a sad state of affairs. His mother was in a serious condition of ill health, his brother Joe had broken his hip, and there was no one to nurse or attend to the farm but his sister Sallie and his father, who was opposed to Bob's enlistment. As usual, Bob Walker turned to his home duties without question.

As the months passed, and more and more of his friends enlisted, Bob became very restive under the parental stand against enlisting. Finally he secured his father's permission to seek advice from a family friend in Alexandria. Armed with his father's letter of introduction, he boarded a train on the newly completed Alexandria & Orange Railroad. At the small town of Manassas, the train was stopped by the exciting news that there had been a battle and the passengers might visit the battlefield if the train would wait long enough. Farmers with wagons were accepting 25¢ per passenger to take sightseers to the battlefield.

Once there, this sightseer needed only one glance to add the final touch to his decision. Dead men and horses, broken rifles and shattered equipment littered the seared ground. Two dead soldiers, their features swollen by the merciless sun, lay twisted in each other's arms. Bob Walker recognized the face of one of his college friends. He did not need to consult the family friend in Alexandria. He enlisted in General Johnston's outfit.

He "had no elbow room", as he expressed it, in the close formation of infantry drills, so when Col. John S. Mosby told General Stuart that with one hundred men he could keep one hundred thousand Yankees guarding Washington, the command known as "Mosby's Rangers" was created by General Stuart, and Bob Walker joined them. He later became Captain of Company B, the youngest Captain in Mosby's remarkable outfit. He had a few narrow escapes, including being shot through the stomach and left to die, as the wound looked fatal. However, his comrades finally came back for him in a spring wagon, took him home and got a doctor, who opined, "He must have been leaning forward, and his stomach must have been mighty empty." At any rate, no vital organs were affected, and Bob Walker was soon in the field again.

His return home after the War was over has been described

Robert S. Walker, captain in Mosby's Rangers of the Confederate Army.

hundreds of times in the experiences of every other Southerner who was not killed on the battlefield. Devastation of everything – the land, the personal possessions and the human spirit – was the heritage of those who had given their bodies to be burned. Captain Bob's brother Joe had died; one sister had died on her wedding journey; his mother was dying; the whole of beautiful "Rosni" was devastated; his father was desperate. Many of Bob Walker's friends had gone west to begin again. Others gave up and dragged their families to the bottom. Typical of him, Bob Walker, who had never done any real work in his life before he joined the Army, pitched in and started a task which was carried into the next two generations of his family – that of helping to build a new South on its funeral pyre.

For the next seven years he worked as a farmhand without pay and brought "Rosni" back into a good state of cultivation. During this time, his mother died and his father remarried. Only Captain Bob and his sister Sallie were left when they received another reward.

One morning Bob and Sallie found their father's present to them beside their breakfast plates: the deed to Woodberry

Forest, a farm of 250 acres lying a few miles to the east of "Rosni" and recently purchased from the family of William Madison, brother of James Madison of "Montpelier", fourth president of the United States. In 1872, Bob and Sallie moved over to the hundred-year-old house which Madison termed "The Residence" in his will. Apart from his more famous brother, William Madison was a man of some distinction of his own making. According to "Saint-Memin in Virginia" by Fillmore Norfleet, he was born May 1, 1762, in Orange County, son of James Madison, Sr. of Montpelier and his wife, Eleanor Rose Conway. He was educated at William and Mary College, where he was one of the original members of Alpha Chapter of Phi Beta Kappa, initiated in 1780. He served in the Revolution as Lieutenant-Colonel and studied law under Thomas Jefferson who, family legend says, designed "The Residence," which Madison built ten years after his marriage in 1782 to Frances Throckmorton of Culpeper County. William Madison served in the Virginia legislature during 1806-07, and while in Richmond had his portrait executed by the French artist, Saint-Memin. A visitor to Montpelier in 1809 writes that she met Mr. Madison, his wife and several near relatives, "all plain country people, but frank, kind, warm-hearted Virginians."

Woodberry Forest had suffered even greater devastation than had "Rosni", which meant that Bob Walker began his work of reclamation all over again. By the end of a year, Bob had started still another career for himself. He courted and, in January 1874, married charming little Anne Carter Goss (called Nannie), the daughter of Ebenezer Goss of "Somerset House" at Somerset, Virginia, twelve miles from "Woodberry Forest" in neighboring Orange County. Her schooling in New Orleans, where she roomed with her first cousin Mary Nalle, had given her a culture and a cosmopolitan outlook on life accorded few girls of that day. As Captain Bob drove his bride

Anne Carter Goss who became the wife of Captain Walker and the mother of six sons for whose education Woodberry Forest School was founded.

up to "The Residence", his sister Sallie greeted them at the front door, and handed the keys to the new mistress of the house. From that time on until Sallie's death, eighteen years later, no friction between these two women was ever noted.

The birth of John Carter Walker on November 12, 1874 was the beginning of a responsibility which Captain Bob accepted with the same kind of deference to the inevitable that he always felt. By the time another decade had passed, Captain Bob and "Miss Nannie" had six sons: John Carter, Joseph Goss, John Scott, Robert Stringfellow, Jr., Frank Stringfellow and Albert Stuart, all born about two years apart.

The First Four Walker Boys, about 1883.
Left to right: Robert Walker Jr., John Walker,
Carter Walker, Joseph G. Walker.

Names for the sons was a live subject. The eldest was christened John for his grandfather Walker, and Carter for his mother's middle name; the second was Joe, for his uncle on the Walker side, and Goss, his mother's family name; Miss Nannie gave in at the third christening and the child was named John Scott, for his paternal grandfather; the fourth became Robert Stringfellow, Jr., without argument. But when it came to the christening of the fifth son, the minister, the Rev. Frank Stringfellow, General Lee's famous scout and a distant relative of the Walkers, had taken the child in his arms before the family had decided what his name should be and intoned "I christen thee Frank Stringfellow," thus naming the child for himself. At the christening of the sixth boy, Cousin Frank, who had christened all the children except Carter, turned to the child's mother and said, "Nannie, it's your turn. I will give this child any name you wish." Accordingly he was named Albert after her greatly admired uncle Albert Nalle, and Stuart – no one is quite sure after whom, but at least, the Stuart is spelled as it was in General J. E. B. Stuart's name.

The question of their schooling was one which eventually turned a simple family history into the fascinating saga of a great educational institution.

It all began with the simple fact that there were no schools in the neighborhood to which Miss Nannie was willing to send her boys. For her first-born, Carter, the whole issue had been settled on the day John, the third son, was born. Sallie, whom the boys were to call "Aunt Mit", walked into Miss Nannie's room and said, "Nannie, you have too many children; I'll take Carter." From that time on Carter began to earn the nickname his brothers always used, "King of Men". He did his lessons with Aunt Mit and when the house was done over in 1884, Carter was given the "little room" that had been the pantry and was next to Aunt Mit's. Carter was the only one of the children who ever had a room to himself, says Mr. Joe, the second brother and chronicler of the family. "As small boys, Frank and Stuart slept in a trundle bed that was pushed under their parents' bed during the day. In later days they'd laugh and say, 'We never had any place we could call our room except a hamper for our clothes'."

Aunt Mit having taken charge of Carter, Miss Nannie undertook to teach the other children. "She would often be holding a baby in one arm, patting the butter with the other hand, and have a book propped up in front of her from which she was hearing the spelling lesson of one of the boys," Mr. Joe recalls. This could not go on indefinitely, and the next move was that Miss Nannie engaged her unmarried sister, Lottie, to come and take over the lessons. This worked fairly well for two years, except when Lottie's beaux turned up. Then "school" just closed for the time being.

The actual beginning of Woodberry Forest as a school could be set in September 1887 when Miss Bessie Grinnan, the eldest daughter of Dr. Andrew J. Grinnan of "Brampton" (the adjoining place to Woodberry Forest), came to teach the four oldest Walker boys, Carter, Joe, John and Rob, and brought her younger sister, Georgia, as a student. A room was fitted up as a school room and "Miss Bessie" walked over each morning. On rainy days, the three older boys went over to the Grinnan house for school. Rob was delicate and too young for the walk, so he just missed those days.

Of Miss Bessie, Mr. Joe says, "She gave us training that was rare indeed for those days. From her, we boys learned far more than ever could be gotten from books. Each day when school was over and she was ready to walk home, she'd manage to have one or two of the boys walk a little way with her, and it was then that they all unconsciously received those groundings in character that were to mean much to them later."

Miss Bessie was forced by ill health to retire at the end of her second year of teaching and the school year of 1889-1890 opened with a full-fledged teacher, J. Thompson Brown, in charge of eight students. The four Walker boys and Georgia Grinnan had been now joined by Brown's younger brother, Willie, Lewis Williams, son of John G. Williams of Orange, and Vivian Slaughter, grandson of the Walker family physician. For the 19-year-old teacher and his eight pupils, the Marye Cottage, built behind "The Residence" by Mr. Madison for his son-in-law and daughter, was fitted up as a dormitory and classroom building.

Of this first year, Lewis Williams has written: "The teacher was new to his work, but Capt. and Mrs. Walker continued in the way they had brought up their own boys. Mrs. Walker watched over the two youthful boarders with the same motherly care she gave her own sons. She even took pains to see that they did not kick off the covers at night. Capt. Walker held daily family prayers for the household and took the whole school with him to St. Thomas' Episcopal Church in Orange on Sundays.

"From the beginning, a standard of thoroughness and hard work was established at the school. Thompson Brown started off with a long list of rules, with demerits for their breach, suggestive of a modern bureau of government. These he soon abandoned for general discipline requirements. It is believed that Captain Bob determined upon this change of method. By simple rules in the art of living, developed through his experience in the midst of devastation on the battlefields of Virginia, Captain Bob added something, year by year, to school discipline. If there was anything in which he was outstanding, it was in encouraging boys not to be afraid. He taught them that it was as important not to overrate the difficulties of a task as to underrate them. A favorite saying of his was—'Boys, the enemy's powder is as wet as yours.' Sometimes he would whoop it up with a crowd of boys; at another, he would quietly take a boy off to himself and help clear up that boy's difficulties. He had the bedside manner of a good family physician, and when a boy was indisposed, he would administer some of the old-fashioned remedies. Mrs. Walker watched tenderly over the boys and gave many a one thoughtful advice about his work and conduct in the school. Her admonition was effective because it was animated by interested concern and was always considerate."

The second year of this little school began with a vast increase in students. New boys included Edmund and Lawrence

The first Student Body on the steps of "The Residence". First row: Mrs. Walker, Captain Walker, Rev. Flournoy Bouldin. Second row: Alex Nelson, Dan Willcox, John Walker. Third row: Thomas Moore, Alan Murray, A. Dibrell, Carter Walker, Lawrence Lee, Edmund Lee, unidentified. Fourth row: William Brown, Rebecca Brown, Eustace Golsan, Lewis Williams, William Booton, Logan Golsan. Fifth row: Stuart Walker, Vivian Slaughter, Miss Janie Slaughter, Frank Walker.

Lee, Eustace and Logan Golsan, William Rust from Loudon County and William Wilcox from the south side of the James River. The third year saw even greater expansion. A two-story house was built across from the Marye Cottage, with schoolrooms on the lower floor and bedrooms for the boys on the second floor. Flournoy Bouldin and Lindsay Marshall were the teachers that year, Thompson Brown having asked for a leave of absence to complete his education. There were twenty-four pupils at the school in 1892-93. First to graduate were J. Carter Walker, Lewis C. Williams and William C. Brown, the school's inveterate prankster. Carter Walker decided to enter West Point, for which he was examined, but from which he was debarred when it was discovered that his eyesight was too deficient to allow him to take military training. He returned to Woodberry for a post-graduate course, and with Edmund Lee left the following year in 1894 for the University of Virginia. Of the first four Woodberry Forest alumni, all were now in college, and with the exception of Brown, who did not stay to graduate, all received their Master of Arts degrees, in three years. A significant detail is that in 1897, the University of Virginia awarded nine Master of Arts degrees. Three of them were won by three of the first four graduates of Woodberry Forest.

In 1896, with three teachers and fifty-three students on roll, Captain Bob issued the first catalogue of "Woodberry Forest High School". Tuition was $255., and included also "board, fuel, laundry, lights and mending." Outlined courses included English, Physics, Mathematics, Latin, Greek, French and German. It was stated that the school was "select and limited. As there are few, of course more attention can be devoted to each student and his character can be the better studied. We do not desire boys who do not have sound morals and studious habits. Every boy is made to feel perfectly at home and is treated as a member of the family."

Chapter II

GROWING PAINS

THOMPSON BROWN left the little school the following year, 1897, to become associated with another school. When it became apparent that a number of the students were going with him, Capt. and Mrs. Walker were greatly disturbed. They had started this school and had boosted its enrollment to such a sizeable figure that it seemed impossible to abandon the undertaking now. Carter had just graduated from the University of Virginia. His father and mother prevailed upon him to remain at home just one year as head teacher to get the little school re-established on a sure footing. It was typical of Carter's nature that his respect for his parents' wishes superseded any ideas of his own. Not only did he agree to come back and work in the little home school for a year, but he brought with him his old schoolmates: Willie Brown, brother of the withdrawing Thompson, and Dalton Dillard. As a special tribute to the sacrifice of his son's ambition to study law, Captain Bob termed the 23-year-old Carter "Head Master". That 1897 catalogue was in other ways significant of the path of the future. The name of M. A. Turner, a dominant influence in the building of the School, appeared for the first time as a master. All the textbooks were changed and the course of study considerably enlarged. "Sacred Studies" appeared as one of the courses and the Rev. Frank Stringfellow's name appeared as chaplain.

Up to this point, Woodberry Forest had been a backyard school on a post-war Virginia farm. That kind of set-up has special social and practical qualities which are almost unique in the history of this country, and it seems logical to take a short backward glance in this narrative in order that the reader may picture for himself the atmosphere in which this somewhat unique educational venture had germinated and was now growing.

How to run a farm in an impoverished state without private means, to say nothing of the lack of government subsidies, was the question facing Captain Bob when he took over Woodberry Forest in the first place, seven years after General Lee had surrendered at Appomattox.

The earliest picture of the Woodberry Forest School baseball team. Joe Walker was manager and Carter Walker played first base. Back row: J. G. Walker, A. G. Murray, W. G. Brown, A. Dibrell, Logan Golsan. Front row: W. S. Booton, L. C. Williams, F. Bouldin (Master), Eustace Golsan, J. C. Walker.

By the time Captain Bob had six sons, he had got the place going pretty well with the help of a few faithful Negro servants, but it never occurred to him to let things stop there. He believed that as each boy became old enough, he should have regular jobs geared to his age and aptitudes. Pulling weeds, watering the stock, churning and other such homely chores were regularly allotted the Walker boys, the other students, and the little colored children growing up on the place with them. As they all grew up, they began helping with the heavier work, which included harvesting, building, planting and all the rest.

It takes imagination to realize the primitive nature of even gracious living in those days. The oil lamps and their care was just an example. Aunt Mit took over this task to relieve Miss Nannie of one more chore. There were fifteen lamps. They were collected in one place each day and Aunt Mit would then trim the wicks, fill the lamps with oil, and wipe the completed job perfectly dry; for oil lamps and later oil stoves were a fire hazard of the first magnitude.

When the boys were old enough, getting the family to church in Orange became a real problem. There was a buggy, but some of the family must go on horseback, using the gentle workhorses, with the small boys riding double, the smaller boy behind. Capt. Walker's riding horse, Corez, had refused to carry double, but one Sunday morning the Captain determined to put up with that no longer. So getting all set in the saddle, he had one of the men lift John, then a little fellow, up behind him. Corez looked around and showed the whites of his eyes but did not move until Capt. Walker touched him with a switch. Then that horse put on a bucking show and Capt. Walker a skill at riding that would have done credit to a Western rodeo.

The first time Rob, Jr., was taken to church he would not sit still, finally turning completely around, and seeing Katie

"The Residence" during one of the annual teas on the lawn before graduation day. Boys and girls listen to a concert by the orchestra which will play that evening for the Final Dance.

Williams, a little girl about his age with golden curls, two seats back of him, he was fascinated. Whispering audibly, he said, "Mother, can't I have it to take home with me?" Kate always said it was her first proposal.

In those days, the boys were often taken by their father on rabbit-tracking expeditions when it snowed. Captain Bob took his army pistols along and shot the sitting rabbits through the eye "to keep from bruising them and ruining the meat", he said. Fresh meat was a rare treat, for there were no markets in Orange.

At last, in 1884, Captain Bob and Miss Nannie felt they could afford to remodel "The Residence". A local man (Os Bridwell) who was a good carpenter, but "with no head at all", as Captain Bob used to say, was engaged for the job. He was just employed by the day for $1.50. He got the other carpenters and helpers.

There was no place where bricks and mortar could be bought, so the carpenter made up a bill of lumber, and trees were cut and sawed on the place. A kiln was started to dry and season the lumber. Another crew dug a cellar under the one-story house, hauling the Virginia red clay a safe distance down the hill where it was burned into bricks to build the present basement walls under the house.

A large cow barn went up in 1885 and neighbors were asked to come for a "barn raising", something new for this neighborhood. They were rewarded by the remarkable sight of each side of a big barn being lifted by hand power, secured in position, then framed to its adjoining sides – all in one day.

The dairy under the dwelling was finished and the barn was built, but there were few cows to furnish the milk, so Captain Bob determined to buy them from farmers. He soon found that statements given by their owners of how much milk each cow gave, its butter fat content, and other statistics, could not be relied upon, so he himself had to watch each cow being milked morning and night, spending much time compiling his records. Payments were so slow in coming from the Richmond firms to whom cream and butter were being sold, that Captain Bob found it necessary to go there once a month to collect payments.

It is almost impossible to realize the handicaps, hardships and discouragements under which Captain Bob and Miss Nannie struggled through these days of the 1880's. There was no bank nearer than Fredericksburg and there were almost no usable roads in winter. The public roads in the entire section had only one man regularly employed on each, the remainder of the work being done by the property owners themselves, each man giving two days a year of his own personal labor or that of his paid employee.

This was the kind of wholesome atmosphere in which the little school grew up. And yet, in the big house, the growing family of boys of both home and school ate well at Miss Nannie's bountiful table — even if they were called the "skimmed milk boys" by neighbors who learned of Captain Bob's success in selling his cream in Richmond. Besides, they had all the cultivation that human spirits need, including religious studies at the hands of Miss Nannie herself, medical attention from the capable hands of Dr. Thomas Slaughter, learning from able scholars, athletics which included everything from snowballing to spirited baseball games with the neighbors, and lovely young ladies to visit in nearby homes, even if they did have to ford the river to do so. All of it was a great adventure.

Encouraged by the continued growth of the school, despite the fact that Mr. Brown had taken about one-third of the student body with him when he left for his new situation, Captain Bob decided to expand the venture into a building and plant properly suited to its intellectual output. When the plan became known in the neighborhood, Captain Bob and Miss Nannie were besought by relatives and friends not to undertake it. John G. Williams, Captain Bob's friend and lawyer, told him, "Bob, don't get into debt at your age" (Captain Bob was then 58). Nevertheless, Captain Bob and Carter went to the Episcopal High School and consulted Dr. Blackford, whose kindness and help to the young headmaster during the ensuing years should be a treasured memory to all interested in Woodberry Forest.

Dr. Blackford suggested a consultation with Dr. Endicott Peabody, who had just started Groton School in Massachusetts patterned after the English Schools. Thither went Captain Bob and Carter. Dr. Peabody placed at their disposal information of every sort about his school and how it was run, and offered to serve the new school in any way he could, including extending an invitation to the new School's architect to visit Groton, as he did. However, Mr. Walker still maintains that

Rear view of the Main Building as seen from the long path to "The Residence." The picture was taken shortly after the building was erected in 1899.

"Dr. Peabody told us nothing to encourage us," but the friendship between these two titans of education continued through Dr. Peabody's lifetime and was instrumental in drawing Mr. Walker into the select circle known as The Headmasters Association of America.

With all this to fight, not to speak of the elements, Captain Bob mortgaged his property to the hilt for $30,000, and in 1898 started to build for the future on a monumental debt and a hill of red Virginia clay. "Captain Bob is crazy", the neighbors said, and there may have been times when the family also wondered about it.

There had already been as much controversy about the location of this building as there had been about the decision to erect it. The first thought was to situate it on the hill north of "The Residence". One day Joseph Wilmer, a neighbor, came for dinner. He stood on the front porch of "The Residence" and pointed straight ahead of him to the southwest. "There is where the school must be built", he said, "right where that oak tree stands."

Mrs. Walker was horrified. "Mr. Wilmer, you would not put a schoolhouse in front of my residence?"

"Mrs. Walker," he replied, "the day will come when people will look out of the back windows of the School and ask, 'Who lives in that little house down there?' " In recent years, that has often happened.

John Minor Botts Lewis, a distant cousin and a young architect from Lynchburg, was engaged to draw the plans. Because of the limited funds, it was first decided to build only the center section and one wing, but when the foundations were being laid, Captain Bob insisted that both wings emanating from the center section be erected. Where the money was coming from, he could not know. There was enough then for only the center section and one wing. Suitable clay for making bricks was found on the property and a kiln erected for their manufacture. (This kiln later made the bricks even for the gymnasium erected in 1939). Lumber which had already been cut on the place was stacked in the kilns for drying. A stunning blow came when much of this timber was burned, and second-rate timber had to be substituted. It became necessary to buy a traction engine to haul the bricks and lumber to the building site.

Just after the building was well started, Mr. Joe's health broke down and it was necessary to send him on a long sea voyage. During that time, the young headmaster was carrying on the academic department in the little buildings behind "The Residence" and was also wrestling on the new one with the workmen, who threatened on one occasion to withdraw because word got around that there was no money to meet a certain payroll. The rumor was true and Mr. Carter Walker knew he had to get the money somehow, beause the building had to be finished. He telegraphed his cousin Fanny (Mrs. Frank Aglionby), a staunch friend and admiring relative, to wire him $5,000 on loan. The request was immediately granted, the work proceeded, and the loan eventually repaid. But the money gave out again after the $5,000 from Mrs. Aglionby tided them over. Captain Bob set out to call on friends and relatives in the neighborhood to ask for help with his continuing financial problems. With no security of any kind, he managed to scrape together enough in friendly loans to get the building ready for occupancy in February 1899.

Hardly had the fifty-five boys and five masters moved into the Main Building, as they called the Walker Building then, when they were cut off from the outside world by the worst blizzard ever recorded in Northern Virginia. When the three feet of snow eventually melted, the Main Building stood in a sea of mud and there was no money left for anything but sawdust walks, which, much later, gave way to board planks filled in with sawdust. It was years before the school could afford brick paths and the long cement walk to "The Residence".

But the lighting and heating were the marvel of the neighborhood; a model student government organization was in successful operation; college entrance requirements were being prepared for in every classroom; entrance examinations were already in use for placement and aptitude; the farm was producing all the food set forth on the still bountiful table; and the five remarkable men who composed the faculty covered every course in the curriculum: J. Carter Walker, the headmaster, taught English and History; Mortimer A. Turner, his right hand in many phases of school life for many years, taught French and German; Clinton M. Kilby taught all the mathematics and the sciences; Dr. J. B. Browder taught Greek and Latin; and the school chaplain, the Rev. Frank Stringfellow, taught sacred studies. Robert Stringfellow Walker was listed in the catalogue as Principal; Joseph G. Walker as proctor; and Mrs. Lizzie Mosby as matron.

By the time the 1904 catalogue was issued, the basic structure of the school was complete. The last Walker boy, Stuart, or "Sixie", as they called him, was a member of the student body; John Walker had completed his college course and was director of athletics as well as teacher of Greek and Mathematics; scholarship medals were being awarded at Commencement; the Oracle (the school paper) and the choir were outstanding extra-curricular activities; Mr. Carter Walker had married the enchanting Harry Hurt of Nashville in 1900 and was the father now of two children, Coleman Carter and Helen Pendleton (Bob was born later); and the remarkable Woodberry Forest-Episcopal High School football rivalry, which, today, is said to be the longest unbroken football series among American preparatory schools, was two years old.

The physical aspect of the school grew commensurately. As originally erected with its central portion and two wings ex-

A group of Woodberry Forest boys in 1911 showing off Mr. Walker's E.M.F. ("Every Mechanical Failure").

tending to east and west, the Walker Building outgrew itself in five years. By 1904 its central section was extended toward the north to enlarge the dining room. A year later, the west wing was crossed by another wing running from north to south, and in those early days termed "The gym wing," as the athletic department was housed there. In another five years, a matching wing was added to the east side of the building; it contained the Headmaster's study and Mr. and Mrs. Walker's apartment, where they lived for the remainder of their Woodberry lives. Cottage C, a beautiful little brick building, was built in 1907 right behind the Walker Building. For some years it was Mr. and Mrs. R. W. D. Taylor's and Mr. and Mrs. Robert Fetzer's dwelling. Boys lived on the second floor and the masters in the two apartments below. It is still called "Old Taylor" in memory of two of its denizens, and the Lords' house, built in 1921, may be called Cottage D, but its real name to most Woodberry-ites is "The Tabernacle".

By far, the most significant and dramatic piece of building was the road and bridge across the Rapidan River, which hastened the future development of the school. It was discovered that the regularly used route to Madison Mills, a road which was often made impassable by the weather, was considerably longer than one which would follow the Rapidan, cross it, and cut through the Wambersie property to the main road. The negotiations to acquire rights for the latter purpose were concluded successfully after some time and trouble. Even with this much preparation, however, Mr. Walker and Mr. Joe were much startled by Captain Bob's pronouncement to them in 1904 that he was going to start to build a road.

His two sons at once began to argue. They had borrowed every cent that the credit of the school could stand or that they thought they could ever repay, and it was unthinkable that they could raise the money which the road and bridge would cost.

"All my life", their father retorted, "when I have found myself faced with a decision which I did not know how to make, I have taken my problem to my Creator in prayer. I have done that in this instance and have emerged from the experience with the conviction that I shall undertake this work with the approval of Our Lord."

Joe looked at Carter and asked the obvious question, "What are you going to do with that argument?" After some private conferring, the sons told their father that they did not doubt "that the Lord has plenty of money, but the only conclusion we can come to is that if he should fail to mete it out, we shall have to come up with it."

Captain Bob withered them with his reply, which both remember to this day: "What you young men lack is a thing that I predict will undermine any success you may have in life; and that is a faith in Almighty God."

The road was put into construction, beginning off the main highway and circling behind the present laundry to the ford. What Captain Bob was planning was the present route in front of the laundry and a bridge over the river, but the work was getting close to the ford when something happened.

About 1906, Captain Bob was seated by the road watching the men at work on his pet project, when Joseph Bryan of Richmond drove by on the way to see his sister, Mrs. Grinnan, at "Brampton". The two men greeted each other cordially, as they had been comrades in arms in the days of Mosby's Rangers. The Brampton Grinnans had used the Woodberry Forest road through a family understanding that never even included an easement.

"Bob", said Mr. Bryan, "what on earth are you doing here?"

"Building a road."

"And what are you going to do when you get to the river?"

"Build a bridge."

"Have you got the money?"

"No, but I hope I can get it."

"Bob," said Mr. Bryan, "when I get to Richmond, I am going to write you a check."

It came, that check (for $3,500), perhaps meted out by Almighty God. Mr. Joe says that when his father showed it to him, he said, "Son, here's your check; now, where's your faith?" And both sons say that Captain Bob never failed to point the moral. He also never failed to remark the fact that the new road got his tomatoes to the Orange market in thirty instead of in sixty minutes.

A laundry loomed as a necessity. Ever since the days when the school was in the backyard of "The Residence", the laundry had been done by local Negro women. Now there was too much work for that method. The enterprising business manager, Mr. Joe, also noted the fact that since Orange had no laundry to which the school could send its work, a school laundry could get work from Orange. It is one of Mr. Joe's special talents to kill two birds with one stone. The site was a question. The river bank down by the new bridge seemed a likely spot, so Mr. Joe took himself to Fredericksburg to consult Mr. Booker T. Marshall, the owner, as to how much he considered to be worth the small rocky point between the branch and the river.

"Worth?" said Mr. Marshall in amazement. "Never saw it but once and that was when I bought the place. You go home and tell Bob Walker to cut off from my tract along there what he needs for the laundry, have a deed drawn, and I will sign it. You will have to pay me a dollar to make the title legal, but I'm glad of a chance to help with that fine school."

Doubtless, Captain Bob began pointing the moral again. The laundry was built and has been a valuable school asset ever since.

One more enterprise took a significant place in the moral and physical upkeep of the school, and that was the summer inn business. Captain Bob and certain ones of his sons, have a perfect genius for turning their own need into a public benefit. Back in the days when the boys were little and the farm just beginning to flourish, it became a regular thing for Richmond friends and relatives of Captain Bob and Miss Nannie to pay them long summer visits. Woodberry Forest was a perfect place for a summer holiday. There was the magnificent table supplied with the delicious fresh vegetables, and fresh milk right off the farm; there was a beautiful river to bathe in; and there were six handsome and eligible young men always ready with their attentions to the lucky ladies. (Amazingly enough, the system still has not changed much; about the only difference being that the summer school now usually enrolls about eighty young men.)

At any rate, Mr. Joe was chiefly thinking that the summer recess could damage what had been built up during the School session: servants would disperse and buildings deteriorate, as such idleness was no better for equipment than for human beings. Against his mother's wishes ("I do not want my sons 'taking boarders'. Besides, you will never succeed, and my boys must not fail at anything"), Mr. Joe started rounding up his summer business and hastily readying something like a golf course by giving the cows a lusher pasture for the time being. With a bountiful table, plenty of old-fashioned Negro servants, and all kinds of comfortable diversions, people came from all over and have never stopped. Eventually it became an academic necessity to operate a summer school session, which has run concurrently with the Inn's season.

These were the beginnings, based as are all beginnings on experimentation and high hopes; beset with struggles and mistakes; but in this case bolstered by courage and loyalty.

Chapter III

MEN, WOMEN AND IDEALS

IT SEEMS LOGICAL to stop for a moment to look at Woodberry Forest's great personalities, not only the Walkers, but many others associated with them in the formative years. There was hardly a member of the school community in those early days who was not a study in his own right.

Of Captain Bob, his son, Carter, says: "Father was a man of abounding energies, profoundly religious, and a man whom other men looked up to and followed readily. He was in no way a man of letters; he was quick-tempered and subject to seizures of deep depression of spirit. He was an entirely lovable person and my devotion to him had no limit." Governor Kemper, a neighbor, often said of him, "Mr. Walker is a fine man, but he will never succeed – he is always in a hurry."

Although afflicted with night blindness, he never allowed this handicap to interfere with his activities, and even during the war, when he was called upon to make extended night raids with the Rangers, he often admitted that he had to leave much to his horse. His marksmanship was extraordinary despite his limited vision, and many a boy has admiringly watched him while he took shots, more often than not with his army revolver, at birds perched in the tops of the tallest trees. His physical prowess on horseback, on the farm and in school games made him a heroic figure in the eyes of the boys. His strikingly powerful voice could be lifted up to summon anyone from anywhere on the place. One alumnus can imitate it perfectly now when he remembers how Captain Bob would stand on the porch of "The Residence" and call the school

The portrait of Mrs. Robert S. Walker.
(Painted by Rosamond Niles.)

The portrait of Captain Walker.
(Painted by Rosamond Niles.)

boys from the Main Building, a good three hundred yards away, 'Ooooooooohhh, Boys! Bring your laundry bags". The bags were filled with apples, which Captain Bob kept by the wagon load, stored in the basement.

When he came out on the porch and sat down, placing the Bible on his knees, everybody knew that some boy was in trouble—of his own making. When one of the school boys was sick, Captain Bob's bedside manner and practiced hand with home-made remedies were those of the best physician. His ideas of discipline became the keynote of the school's Honor System; pranks he would tolerate, but owning up to them straightforwardly and unafraid, was adamantine.

Captain Bob's naturalness and lack of affectation are signified by this little story told by Mr. Joe: "Carter Walker was interviewing Mr. and Mrs. John Doe about sending their son to Woodberry Forest. The young headmaster was trying to make the proper impression on these exceedingly desirable patrons and obviously cultivated persons when Captain Bob, whose middle name was ubiquitousness, strolled in. After listening for a moment to Carter's high-flown description of his high purposes, during which he remarked that although the school was young, the standards were high and the boys had to work, Captain Bob chimed in with, 'Yes, it's root hog or die with us.' The poor headmaster almost expired with embarrassment and later told his father, 'You mustn't say things like that. People won't understand.' 'Well,' returned the Captain, 'they entered Jimmie, didn't they?' "

Something like the end of an era came in 1914 with Captain Bob's death. Mr. Joe has thus touchingly recorded the details of that event:

"It was the 31st of January, 1914. All hands were busy harvesting ice. Captain Bob had been at the pond since early morning, but left to attend the funeral of Wilson, who had for many years been one of the most trusted colored men on the farm. When he returned, he went back to the ice pond, directing that his dinner be sent to him there.

"On retiring that night, he said to the small Negro boy who waited on him, 'Carroll, my feet are cold. Bring me two bottles of hot water.' The water was too hot and the next morning both feet were badly burned, one more so than the other. His diabetes had kept Captain Bob from feeling the intensity of the heat. The burns kept him bedfast for some time.

"The Rev. Bob Carter, rector of the Episcopal Church in Orange, was a frequent visitor at the bedside. The patient was not improving, and one day, Mr. Carter said, 'Let me see those burns.' When he had removed the bandages and taken a look, he called the family and burst forth with, 'What's the matter here? Don't you know that gangrene has set in on both of Bob's feet? He should be gotten to the hospital at once.'

"The train was the only means of conveyance to Charlottesville and arrangements to transport the patient thereby were quickly made. While the family was waiting at the railroad station in Orange, Ben Bowler, the barber, came from his shop up the street and cut the Captain's hair.

"At the University hospital, the doctors informed the family that the only hope for saving Captain Bob's life lay in removing the leg above the knee. When consulted, Captain Bob insisted that he was 'too old and too heavy for that.' He asked that the amputation be made at the ankle. As the doctors feared at the time, this operation did not suffice, and Captain Bob died on Saturday, March 14, 1914. His three eldest sons and their wives were standing around the bed when the end came. Dr. John Staige Davis folded the Captain's arms over his chest, and the family quietly left the room.

"On Sunday, the body was brought to Orange and placed in St. Thomas' Church. Masters from the school took turns at the 'watch' through the night. The next day, the weather was lovely. The whole school and some of the colored servants came to the funeral. The church was packed by these and friends from Richmond and Washington. When the service was over, Cameron Wilson, one of the masters, and the boys took the flowers and marched behind the hearse to the cemetery.

"As the casket was lowered, Miss Nannie dropped to her knees at the foot of the grave. Two of her sons stepped beside her. There was scarcely a dry eye in that gathering—except hers. Then she lifted her head and said, 'Boys, take me home'."

Mrs. Walker, universally known as "Miss Nannie," was a rare spirit — sweet, quiet and determined. She had a gift for keeping things going on a cheerful and efficient basis. She took everything in her stride, but when she put her foot down, it was down for good, and nobody thought of arguing about it. When she was an elderly woman, she remonstrated in her gentle way one day with a young faculty wife for not covering her baby's head. "There is a cold wind blowing today," she smiled. "But, Miss Nannie," protested the young mother, "that is a lovely southern breeze." "My dear," came the determined reply, "don't you know that some of our coldest north winds come from the south?" Once she sweetly remarked to the same friend, "I always get my way, by fair means if possible — if not, by foul." Her ability to handle all kinds of situations was taken more or less for granted by her family, who did not fail, however, to give her credit for saving many a day. Once when she was entertaining at a luncheon party, a special occasion for her who was usually catering to hungry school boys or nursing sick children, old Colonel Mosby turned up unexpectedly. She was a bit nonplussed at this intrusion until the old gentleman sneezed.

"Colonel Mosby," she said, "you have a cold. Now just sit right there and I will bring you a hot toddy. These summer colds can be dangerous." When she appeared with the toddy which she had concocted with regard for its potency, she handed it to him with solicitude: "Now you drink it right down and then go inside and lie down." The Colonel thanked her warmly, downed the toddy and, from its effects, slept peacefully right through the luncheon party.

"Arnold of Rugby never stamped his personality on the boys of that famous English school any more indelibly than J. Carter Walker has stamped his upon those at Woodberry Forest," said the *Richmond Times Dispatch* editorially upon Mr. Walker's retirement as headmaster in 1948. Another editor carries this idea further by observing that "It is not by the mere statement of noble credos that youth was impressed in Arnold's time, nor is it in Mr. Walker's. When the boy is understood, he responds, and a rapport is established in which the coming-of-age process is enriched. It is this long history of mutual understanding that is perhaps the chief ingredient of J. Carter Walker."

If the success of J. Carter Walker can be summarized as easily as the above writers seem to think it can, the character of J. Carter Walker might be interpreted by his words as recorded by his brother Joe: "I always did what Father and Mother told me to." That sense of obedience became the keynote of his administrative career, for which he proved himself to have been unusually gifted. However, Mr. Walker's relationship with the boys is a story all in its own right and has a connotation in the history of the School completely apart from any estimation of Carter Walker, the man and scholar; for the stories which grew up around this titanic, extraordinarily well balanced man in his association with the callow youth entrusted to his care was a legend in its own time.

Without ever being stuffy about it, Mr. Walker's whole approach to his boys was based in his genuine understanding of how to create the atmosphere for a gentleman's agreement. He frequently said, "Honor is a matter of education," and he never lost sight of how honor in growing persons is therefore subject to constant reinterpretation and rebuilding in their understanding. With that sympathy which no boy seems ever to have failed to understand, there was never any barrier to the mutual acceptance of a gentleman's word of honor. Mr. Walker took theirs and they his without an exception and with absolute trust. If that trust was ever violated, it is not a matter of record or recollection. It is significant that no written contract ever existed between the Headmaster and a member of his faculty. A gentleman's agreement sufficed on both sides.

"Woodberry Forest is an unpretentious school," Mr. Walker used to say, and his manners certainly bore out his dictum. Although he was entitled to be called "Dr. Walker" by virtue of his honorary LL.D. degree from Davidson College in 1933, he was addressed only as "Mr. Walker" at Woodberry Forest. Upon his retirement, the University of Richmond also conferred upon him an LL.D. degree, but he is still "Mr. Walker" at Woodberry. He never owned a Phi Beta Kappa key, although his alma mater, the University of Virginia, bestowed that honor upon him.

In the old days when boys lived all around his quarters, their roughhousing would often bring the Headmaster to the end of the corridor, down which he would stride, looking straight ahead, and (because of his peculiar affliction of "gun-barrel" vision) the boys, flattened against corridor doors, knew that he saw no face, but that the situation was well in hand and that nobody better go any further.

The boys had their own code of detection of the Headmaster's approach, which, typical of him in his approach to any kind of situation, was always the opposite of the pussy-foot variety. The rowdies would freeze at the sound of footsteps, and if they could count off, almost on the double, "I-am-J.-Carter-Walker-and-I-am-coming-to-get-you," everyone ran for cover.

He had a nice understanding of the need for balance between work and play, and, as a consequence, was full of toleration for the human being inside each boy. There was the time when Woodberry Forest's glee club was to give an operetta jointly with that of the Warrenton Country School. The evening before, Mr. Walker received a telephone call from the headmistress of that school, who wished to inform the Headmaster that one of her girls had just recovered from a case of mumps; and that although the doctor had pronounced her beyond the contagious stage, Mlle. Bouligny did not wish to bring her without the Headmaster's permission. He replied that she must come by all means, but that he would suggest that the girl avoid unnecessary contact. There was a pause on the other end of the line.

"What would that mean?"

"Well," said Mr. Walker, "I do not know whether the action of the play calls for any kissing, but if so, I would suggest that she refrain from that bit of stage business. Of course, any other kind of kissing would be none of my business."

"What do you mean?" came back in sudden anger.

"My dear madam," Mr. Walker gently replied, "Kissing is a game that boys and girls have been playing for a long time. Have you never heard of it?"

She sputtered back, "You should talk to your boys."

"Any talking of that kind should be done at your end, madam," he returned. "All I can say is that if any one of my boys should have the opportunity to kiss a pretty girl and turn it down, I should be downright ashamed of him!"

In the next breath, he could strip a boy with a memorable diatribe against his irresponsibility, particularly in regard to his studies. Good grades and what it took to produce them occupied Mr. Walker's most earnest consideration at all times. He studied constantly the records of each boy in the School and of those who had graduated from it into college. In his talks with boys about their work, he had each record so well in mind that he was quite able to quote a boy's past grades to him without reference to the files. His fight talks with the laggards at the end of every marking period were frequently more inspiring than they ever were discouraging, although Mr. Walker was not much of a pleader. He simply had a gift for appealing to a boy's own – perhaps dormant – sense of responsibility to himself. One excellent student, who once in his life fell badly behind in his Math, expressed it all by saying, "After my talk with Mr. Walker that time, I felt that I should like to spend the rest of my life working Math problems."

On every one of his associates, young and adult alike, Mr. Walker had the effect of making him wish he were just a little bit better than he knew he was. For that reason, very few boys voluntarily consulted him, but few were ever sorry they had done so. Everything was suddenly perfectly straight in everybody's mind after a conference with the Headmaster.

"I never let a boy leave me aggrieved," Mr. Walker has often said when asked about his experience in getting on with youngsters. "I have frequently followed a boy to his room to talk further when I felt we had not understood each other perfectly." By the same token, he made it a policy never to accept a student at Woodberry Forest, no matter how much his parents wished to send him, until he had the boy's own word that he wished to come.

That respect for a boy's personality took a whimsical turn at times, notably in the case of one youngster whose colorful profanity on the golf course could be heard far enough away to cause complaint from other players. Mr. Walker got hold of the young man.

"Gaines," he said pleasantly, "I suppose I can't keep you from swearing on the golf course, but I am telling you that unless you can keep your profanity on your own fairway, you will have to keep off the golf course. Is that a bargain?"

"Well, I guess so, Mr. Walker," said Gaines after considering the situation, "But I think the bargain is a bit one-sided."

Mr. Walker's dedication to his job of Headmaster left him little time for any of the leisurely pursuits of a less exacting career. When his children were young, he frequently took the boys hunting, even carrying on his back small Bob, too tired to walk home. At that time he was also a tennis player of considerable ability, and for years played every possible afternoon with both masters and boys; during the summers he entered and sometimes won tournaments in Virginia and Maryland. Much of his free time was devoted to self-improvement in reading and studying, which he believed vital to his work. Two summers he spent at the Boston School of Speech, there learning some of the technique which, coupled with his own convictions and talents, made him a masterly rostrum speaker. He also went away for other courses in English literature, although it was perhaps his own God-given talent that made his letters, even the most casual ones, masterpieces of English writing. In his announcements to the school, as well as his other verbal communications, his clever choice of words, including what one master used to call "the crashing negative," could rivet the attention of the most desultory listener. Most of this was the result of constant and lonely study. Once Mrs. Walker left baby Helen to be watched by her father, who was busy as usual with his work. After several interruptions caused by the crawler straying into dangerous places, he nailed her skirt to the floor and resumed his reading in peace.

It was much later in his career that he felt he had time for golf and fishing, although bridge, at which he was a clever and daring player, had been a favorite all along. The arts were entirely outside his realm, yet he was persuaded eventually to include music and art in the school curriculum, and the dramatic club is one of the oldest of the school's extra-curricular activities. The movies were never on his list of diversions.

One day Miss Nina Grinnan telephoned from "Brampton" to tell her friend, Carter, that he must punish two of the school boys who were riding her calves.

"Why certainly, Nina, I shall attend to it immediately. Have you gotten the names of these boys?"

"Yes, I have. They told me they were Clark Gable and Gary Cooper."

"Nina, there is some mistake. We have no boys in the school by those names."

About that time, Ben Finney, an alumnus who has had a rather exotic career, arrived at the school to show off a purple Rolls Royce, in which was riding beside him Miss Barbara LaMarr, then at the height of her cinematic fame. Ben rushed into Mr. Walker's office and urged him to come out to see her. Mr. Walker acquiesced and added, "Ben, it appears that I should be impressed, but who is Miss Barbara LaMarr?"

He treated his faculty in much the same way that he did the boys, knowing instinctively those whom he must curb, those whom he must direct, and those whom he could trust without interference. He knew how to leave personalities entirely out of his relationships. He had a judge's gift for cutting through a mass of detail or a garbled report to the heart of the matter and could often end the whole argument by asking the penetrating question, "What do you think you are here for?," which has a surprising number of applications. The artfulness with which he saw and judged a situation was highlighted by his rapidity in doing so. The waters closed quickly over every hole, leaving no trace.

As an administrator, he was often more severe on the parents than on the boys. Once after a particularly unpleasant encounter with the parents of a boy whose dismissal for illegal smoking had been recommended by the prefects, Mr. Walker thought he had disposed of the matter – a clear case of dis-

J. Carter Walker in 1926.

regard for authority which he never tolerated. A telegram came belatedly from the boy's mother. It was couched in threatening language, demanding "full and explicit information" on the methods used in an alleged unholy session of the prefect board during which, she claimed, a confession of guilt was wrested from the boy by vicious means, and hinting at a suit. There is in J. Carter Walker nothing which may be remotely connected with intimidation.

"Do you know what that means?" he asked his secretary.

"No, sir, I don't," she replied.

"I don't either," he snapped. "Take this telegram in reply: 'Your wire neither intelligible nor courteous. Must be both to be answered'."

Later another boy from the same town was being entered in the school. Mr. Walker, with his usual frankness, suggested that the father of the boy consider this prior incident, in view of the fact that the new boy might be subjected to criticism in his home town because of the earlier unpleasantness.

The man laughed. "Mr. Walker," he said, "I was retained as a legal adviser by the family in that case. After reviewing all the correspondence, I was so impressed by your handling of the matter that I was persuaded this was the school for my son."

His ability to meet a crisis with steely nerves and an unfaltering heart was even more remarkable when it manifested itself in the early days of his headmastership than when he had grown experienced in such junctures. As early as 1902 he was confronted with one of these situations which make it impossible for a popularity seeker to become a headmaster. The School baseball team committed a serious misdemeanor in a hotel in Washington, where the boys had gone, accompanied by masters, to play Georgetown. Later in the evening, high spirits led to strong spirits and before anyone quite knew how it happened, Woodberry boys were drunk and disorderly. The newspaper accounts next day added to the mortification of the School. Mr. Walker speedily wired the parents of every boy known to have been drinking on that occasion to come to the school and remove their son.

A prominent citizen of a nearby city replied by wiring, "If you dismiss my son just before his graduation, I will see to it that no more boys from this city ever go to Woodberry Forest." The wire was not even answered. The boy was dismissed with the others. Many boys have since then come from that city, but the Headmaster could not know the outcome when he took what he considered the only course for the healthy conduct of the School.

Some years later he faced another perplexing moment which might have had a painful conclusion without his deft handling. Mr. Walker had rejected a request from the student body that school be closed in order to allow the students to attend the inauguration of President Wilson. At lunchtime, about fifty boys brought suitcases downstairs and deposited them in the front hall. As soon as grace was said, they rose in a body, collected the suitcases and marched off down the road towards Orange. Whatever his qualms may have been, no one now knows. He spent the rest of the day in his office, directing the masters to await the return of the "strikers" and to give no demerits. Return they did, marching around and into the school building, bearing banners denouncing dictators and advocating freedom and fair play. The masters took Mr. Walker's cue, waved them outdoors to vent their spleen and received them without comment when they returned in time for the evening meal.

No person who has ever been associated with Mr. Walker has failed to receive from him a liberal education in his own field. A secretary to him could have a hard time until she realized she was being given expert coaching in rhetoric and English grammar. "I tell my secretaries," he says, "that I gladly point out a mistake the first time; reluctantly do so a second; and never a third." To the faculty wives he used to say, "Your job is just as important as your husband's." To a mother who was once attempting to obtain a relaxation of the School's discipline of her son for a misdemeanor for which she was trying to take the blame, Mr. Walker barked, "Madam, I should like to suggest to you that this School cannot be administered from 200 homes." When a master attempted to parry a criticism of his performance, the Headmaster drew the interview to a close with, "Young man, I did not ask you to come here to argue with me; I simply tell you that you have made a mistake and I have shown you how to correct it."

Mr. Walker did not consider honesty "the best" policy in dealing with parents: he considered it the only policy. Asked by one parent how he managed to dispose

Thurmond Chatham and J. Carter Walker after a successful hunting trip.

Mrs. J. Carter Walker, painted by Louise Young in 1944, copy presented to The School by a group of Alumni.

The Leopold Seyffert portrait of J. Carter Walker, painted in 1948 and presented to the school by a group of Alumni.

of boys who could not conform to the School standards, he replied,

"Simple. I just tell the parents that the boy is wasting our time and their money. We are much too busy with important things to waste our time on discipline."

When there was a crisis, sometimes involving the Honor System and all its ramifications, Mr. Walker could address the School community with such masterly direction of thinking that no person, adult or youth, could emerge from that gathering without a renewed sense of *esprit de corps,* a tingling conscience, and a stern resolve to do better. On that most dramatic of all graduation days in June 1947, when Mrs. Walker died three hours before the Commencement exercises, Mr. Walker was prepared to go through with the arrangements to the letter until his faculty intervened and cut the exercises to a mere presentation of diplomas. Nevertheless, Mr. Walker took the whole graduating class into the library for a final word. No one else has ever known what that word was, but each one of the fifty lads emerged with streaming eyes.

Close beside him for forty-seven years stood the truly beautiful and always gracious Harry Hurt Walker. She had the diplomacy and the grace of the prototype of the statesman's wife. She knew everything there was to know about J. Carter Walker and his position, and as cleverly knew her place in relation to both.

She was both witty and sweet, a wonderful combination for good company. Once she remonstrated with a master's wife for her overly energetic activities. "My dear," she smiled, "stop going so fast. It is much better for your children to be reared by their own mother than by their stepmother." In fact, she treated boys and grownups alike as her own children. "Mind your manners," she frequently told masters or their wives, "and go speak to the company."

As the fine musician she was, she took special interest in the choir, playing the wheezy old chapel organ, while Mrs. Rawleigh Taylor directed the choir. That was before the time when Woodberry Forest was dignified by a choirmaster or a pipe organ. They do say that the well known Johnny Mercer failed to make the choir, and that the closest he ever got to it was pumping the organ for Mrs. Walker.

Mrs. Walker always gave a choir party during the year, and on one of these occasions she showed much of her greatness. Some of the non-singers decided that this was a good time to have some fun with the choir boys, so it was all arranged that buckets of water were to be placed in the windows above Mrs. Walker's little side porch where the ice cream freezer stood waiting for the moment when one of the singers should be asked to step outside and lift the can out of its cylinder of ice and salt. Everything was ready above and below. One thing went wrong. Mrs. Walker herself stepped outside to attend to the freezer, and Mrs. Walker was doused with two buckets of water. The young gentlemen saw her too late to avoid the catastrophe. They packed their bags, put on their traveling clothes and prepared to leave the school before being asked. But on their way out, they stopped to apologize to Mrs. Walker. She smiled her sweetest, accepted their apology and bade them go back to their rooms. "Let's just keep this between us," she told the culprits. "We won't tell Mr. Walker."

She reared three children in the small dormitory apartment assigned her and Mr. Walker when the Main Building was erected. When its East Wing was built with adequate quarters for the Carter Walker family, Mrs. Walker gaily accepted a false fireplace in her living room because there was not quite enough money to build a chimney. In that living room, she gave Sunday coffee parties for the faculty, during which she played the piano and carried on a running conversation with her guests without missing a beat, musically or conversationally. Into that living room she ushered various and sundry guests in all kinds of trouble from homesickness to school evaluation, usually while some member of the family was in conference with Mr. Walker in his study next door.

She took herself and her sewing to the front hall each morning just to be on hand in case anyone should turn up and wonder where to go. She paid daily visits to the infirmary and spent hours reading to sick boys or just cheering them up. She had a lovely way of putting Mr. Walker in his place when it was her business to do so, and an equally remarkable way of seeming to know nothing about School affairs or community gossip. One of the sincerest tributes any woman could receive was a public one by her husband at a most unexpected moment. Mr. Walker rose in the dining room to make his accustomed remarks to the student body just before the mid-winter dances. After he had reminded the boys of the special rules for conduct during the festivities, he suddenly said, "Let me say that no matter how many beautiful girls will be your guests this week end, or have been here in years past, I have never seen one who could approach Mrs. Walker in beauty, in talent, and in charm when she used to entertain dozens of young men in her sister's home near here."

Joseph Goss Walker was the trouble-shooter of the organization. Illness in his youth prevented him from completing his schooling and kept him so close to home that it was inevitable for him to undertake the management end of the business. In fact, he has remarked that "Mother said I was the only girl she ever had," and it was always his job to see to internal affairs in everything from churning and hog-killing to civil engineering and financing. If he had any other titles than "Boss," which he has always been called, they could be listed as farmer, postmaster, innkeeper, director of the laundry, business manager and personnel director. In his youth, Mr. Joe ran the Orange Milling Company which his father once owned; held the first automobile agency and

The five Walker Brothers in 1954. Left to right they are J. Carter Walker, Joseph G. Walker, John Scott Walker, Frank S. Walker, and Stuart Walker.

owned the first car in Orange and Madison Counties; worked on the first typewriter in the vicinity and was ever on the lookout for the acquisition of adjacent property, or the liquidation of property that was not profitable. His genius for "making do," borrowing from Peter to pay Paul, and keeping extraordinary vigilance over every soul and mechanism on the place was as much responsible for the growth of the school in national reputation as was Mr. Carter Walker's administrative ability—and all with the meagerest of financial resources.

Despite the fact that Mr. Joe's ability was innate and his ingenuity boundless, it is difficult to regard him as an entity after having known "Mrs. Joe."

She was the dynamic, red-headed daughter of an admiral in the United States Navy, born Violet Augusta Cary Niles on the Island of Guernsey. In the summer of 1910, she came to Woodberry Forest as one of the Inn guests, and it was not long before the town of Orange was buzzing with the news that "Joe Walker is going to marry that Navy woman with the big earrings." Miss Niles and her family were then bound for England on a visit to friends. Mr. Joe sailed for England on Christmas Eve of 1910 and he and Miss Niles were married at 11:30 A.M. on January 21, 1911 in St. Pancras' Church in London, where her parents had been married thirty-four years before. Mr. Joe says the hour was selected because the wedding fee would have been doubled had the ceremony taken place thirty minutes later! After a wedding trip to the Continent, during which Mr. Joe picked up enough French to trot it out acceptably forty years later, the Joe Walkers returned to "The Residence," which was to be their home together until Mrs. Joe's death thirty-five years later.

During these years, Mrs. Joe became a tradition in her own lifetime. An executive of the first order, the foundation of her domain was hospitality. An enthusiast for everything pertaining to the welfare of Woodberry Forest, she has turned many a tide and cleverly planted many a seed that created the right atmosphere and determined the best course of action for the whole School. Beneath the elaborately comfortable atmosphere of her home ran the machinery of vast housekeeping operations which included canning the surplus produce from the summer garden for winter use and furnishing meals for the farmhands. A fine horticulturalist, she became third president of the Garden Club of Virginia, a fellow of the Royal Horticultural Society and a contributor to National Horticultural magazines. She did most of the landscaping on the School campus and spent years of painstaking study on the proper plant material for the Piedmont section of Virginia. She filled her house with schoolboys, promoting all kinds of activities among them for the purposes of culture or just plain fun. The School annual and the School book club are two of her permanent creations. Her vivid and lively nature kept everything around her going at top speed, and her enthusiasm and energy transformed every association with her into a memorable experience.

John Scott Walker was at once the athlete and the moderator of the family. Gentility and gentleness are the keynotes of his disposition, and although he served many years as athletic director and as teacher of Greek and head teacher of Mathematics, the athletic activities of the boys were his chief concern for them after his attention to their spiritual and social education. He was forever worrying that books unfit for youngsters to read might find their way into the library, and that they were given insufficient supervision of their winter dress. The building of "The Cage," which was the forerunner of the handsome Alumni Gymnasium, was his special project, even before his crusading activities for the golf course and the tennis courts. He is responsible for having personally directed a number of the most outstanding teachers to the School through his association with a noted boys' camp during the summer months. In his earnest concern for everybody and everything belonging to Woodberry Forest, he became a kind of guardian of the little things that often allow the big things to take care of themselves.

Mr. John married in 1913 the vivacious Marguerite Alden, a Vassar graduate, and a descendant on her father's side of the Mayflower-borne settlers of Massachusetts and on her mother's side of French Huguenots. Dr. Alden, Mrs. John's father, was a college professor of history and a writer of distinction, having contributed to a dozen issues of the Dictionary of American Biography. When the John Walkers were married, Mrs. Joe drew a sketch of the little house which was built for them near "The Residence" and which was similar in design to that house. However, as "Cottage E," it was readapted over the years to the needs of a dozen families and dozens of school boys who have resided there since, so that today the resemblance is rather vague. In time, the John Walkers went to live in the newer "House A," where Mrs. John, in her adaptability to her husband's interests, took charge of the Chapel, entertained hundreds of boys, gave parties for everybody—always the newly arrived masters' wives – and eventually became hostess for the School. Even after she moved to Orange upon her husband's retirement, she never forgot the little, nice compliments which often mean more in morale building than the obviously important ones. Her death in 1953 removed the last of the Woodberry Walker ladies, whose tradition for gracious hospitality is still a real element in the School's personality.

Two of the three younger brothers, Robert S. Jr. and Stuart, were never intimately associated with the growth of the School, as were the others. Rob was a sufferer from asthma, and early in his life moved to California where he lived for many years, married and died. The youngest son, "Sixie" as he was known even through his University of Virginia days, was as outstanding an athlete as his brother John, and lent his talents to many a Woodberry and Virginia team. After acquiring his M. E. and E. E. degrees, he became associated with the General Electric Company, from which he retired in 1953.

Frank S. Walker, the farming genius of the family, acquired by inheritance and purchase his grandfather's place, "Rosni," and went there to live shortly after his marriage to Margaret Shackelford of Orange, a great-great-granddaughter of Thomas Jefferson. Mr. Frank has been for many years president of the Corporation, including the school, farm, dairy and laundry, and was placed there, the family says, in order to maintain the balance of power in the family and to "keep peace" between the three older brothers. A graduate of the Virginia Polytechnic Institute, he has become one of the outstanding farmers of the state.

There are other personalities outside the actual Walker family, but members in good standing of the Woodberry family, who must be catalogued, for their contribution to the building of the School, especially during the formative years, is immeasurable.

Chief among them is the memorable Mortimer Austin Turner, from whom Mr. Carter Walker says he learned as much as he did from his school or his administrative experiences. Mr. Turner had married Miss Nannie's sister, Miss Rosa Goss, and about the time when the Main Building was in construction, he had returned to this country after serving several years as United States consul at St. Thomas' Island in the West Indies. Mr. Turner was persuaded to associate himself with the new School, where he taught modern languages for more than two decades. After he retired from teaching because of his failing eyesight, he remained a dominating figure in the School community until his death in the mid-30's. Many an old boy loves to recall his unique classroom technique which seems to have blended the teaser and the martinet in him with disciplinary effects. His courtliness in his every association can be recalled by everyone, even including wives of his former students. There is one memorable time when a rascal schoolboy conceived the delightful plan of sailing a brimming inkwell down the long hall which ended in Mr. Turner's room. The ensuing mess prompted the Headmaster to warn the student body that whoever was guilty of such a trick was not wanted in the School. That young gentleman got his point, as one never failed to do from one of Mr. Walker's pronouncements, and took himself to Mr. Turner to apologize and beg forgiveness. Mr. Turner's reception of this gesture was so typically magnanimous, that the boy was thereby reinstated in his own self-respect.

Mr. Turner could not sit by and just teach. In the young School and in the growing one, he served in many other capacities, not to speak of that of adviser to the Headmaster. He handled the mail for years before the post office was established, and took upon himself the job of answering the telephone, for neither of which did he receive any extra compensation. He took over the School book store, and from the profits thereof paid off the debt on the Chapel, of which he was treasurer. His unusual talent for writing and speaking the English language and his reverence for its good usage became the inheritance of several generations of Woodberry boys and masters. The boys baited Mr. Turner unmercifully with their crude pronunciations just to enjoy his indignation, but despite all that, they were impressed by his scholarship. The School named its handsome upper-form dormitory building for him. His only daughter, Austin (Mrs. Arthur Jones of Somerset), remains the only female graduate of Woodberry Forest.

In 1909 two men appeared at Woodberry Forest whose influence in their wholly different fields is still as important to Woodberry as it was forty-five years ago.

Rawleigh W. D. Taylor came then to teach Latin, but he did so much more that it would be meaningless to try to describe it. Not only did he teach every little boy, slaving over the slow ones in the evening, but he also took the same personal interest in the education of every new, bumbling master, helping and advising in every department, with special emphasis on having the machinery run smoothly. As the administrator of demerits for many years, Mr. Taylor's long finger of the law, shaken in many a guilty face, has survived more vividly in most memories than Caesar's Gallic Wars. The boys called him "Straw," and the smart cracks on that name rose to flood tide when "The Oracle" commented upon Mr. Taylor's action in closing the Smoke House with the outrageous pun: "Straw Broke The Camel's Back," and christened his newly-born grandson "The Last Straw."

When retirement time came for Mr. Taylor, he decided to assist Mrs. Taylor in her remarkable work with the Alumni Association. At a recent meeting of that body, Mrs. Taylor, the executive secretary, chose a moment when Mr. Taylor had left the room to inform the biennial meeting of the old boys that "Mr. Taylor was just as wonderful in the alumni work as he ever was teaching Latin."

John Embrey, the 19-year-old son of the foreman at "Rosni," arrived also in 1909 to be maintenance man at Woodberry Forest. During his forty-six years in that capacity, he has learned, and now knows, more about Woodberry's physique than any other one person. He has made for the school plant so many accoutrements that it would be impossible to list even the categories. Years ago, when Mrs. Frank Walker took her young son to Richmond to see the statue of General Lee, the child gazed admiringly at the monument and inquired, "Did Don Embry make it, Mama?" "Skeets," as the boys have all called him, has carried the mail, and repaired, renewed or rigged makeshifts for almost every piece of equipment on the place for more than four decades, and has kept everything from going wrong at once by adhering to his colorful dictum, "The squeaking wheel gets the grease."

In the early 1920's, it was discovered that enough mail was coming into Woodberry Forest to justify application for a rural free delivery service. The route was granted and William Graham was appointed mail carrier to the School. However, when the post office department learned that the mail carrier had to open five gates on the route, the service was discontinued. Mr. Joe faced the problem of discovering how to build gates which could be opened without dismounting from the mail carrier's buggy. After a long search and an amusing encounter with a gentleman who was using such a gate, Mr. Joe had five of them built for the School road and the mail route was reinstated. It was not long before Woodberry Forest became a third class post office with Mr. Joe as first postmaster and John Embrey as mail carrier. Eventually Mrs. John assumed that position and she was followed by Mr. Marchant.

Some years ago, when John L. Lewis' son was graduating from Woodberry Forest, Mr. Joe introduced Mr. Lewis to John Embrey, and at once the United Mine Workers' president began to question Mr. Embrey as to how he was being treated from the labor standpoint. In reply, Mr. Embrey informed him that he had never been without a job, had always had enough clothes, plenty of food and a good house. Mr. Embrey says that Mr. Lewis replied, "John, you better stay here. You don't need a union."

In September, 1910 the Rev. Karl Block came to Woodberry Forest as chaplain. A recent graduate of the Virginia Theological Seminary, Mr. Block was young, scholarly and full of enthusiasm. He eventually married Miss Nancy Shackelford, Mrs. Frank Walker's sister, and is now the Episcopal Bishop of California. During the three years he spent at Woodberry, he served ably in many phases of school life. His athletic ability was pressed into immediate service as assistant coach, as well as umpire. His tall, 200-pound figure and his stentorian voice singing "Strike two-o-o-o" became famous in the neighborhood baseball games and ruled out any questioning of his decisions.

At that time, the School had no chapel. All services were held in the public hall. Mr. Block set himself to building a chapel. Pittman Springs, an alumnus, who had been in the school under Mr. Block's tuition, started the ball rolling by giving $1,000. The school Missionary Society collected donations enough to start the building.

The School donated the plot of land on which the Chapel now stands. Mr. Block insisted that the Chapel be church property and belong to the Diocese of Virginia. The School deeded the property to the diocese, but when the Alumni

The Chapel.

assumed ownership of the School in 1926, the diocese deeded the Chapel back to the School, as the building had not been consecrated.

The Chapel was built in 1912-1913. The altar, carved in Italy of Carrara marble, was given by Mrs. John F. Bransford in memory of her son, Alfred, who graduated from Woodberry in 1911 and lost his life later that summer in a vain effort to save his younger brother from drowning.

Until it was returned to the School, the business affairs of the Chapel were managed by three Trustees, Mr. Walker, Mr. Taylor and Mr. Turner. Only Mr. Turner ever knew what the building really cost, for after he assumed its debt (which he paid with bookstore profits) he had the whole financial worry of the charming little brick building he and Mr. Block loved so well.

Some years after the Chapel was built, its original seating capacity of 220 demanded increase by 100 seats. Architecturally, the building could not be enlarged as it stood, and the only solution seemed to be in moving back the chancel end of the building and sandwiching the additional footage between the two sections.

When the architect and builder pronounced this impossible because of certain damage to the beautiful altar, Mr. Joe found a mover who agreed to do the job, but who would accept no responsibility for the result.

Work was begun and a heavy framework was placed under the chancel end, which was then cut loose from the nave. A wooden track was constructed and a capstan placed on the lawn, with its heavy rope fastened to the chapel. A white mule hitched to the capstan completed the operation.

"Start your mule," the foreman shouted. The rope tightened, the timbers creaked and the short section of the building began to move on the small rollers that had been placed under it. In two days, the desired thirty-six feet had been covered. Not one drop of water had been spilled from the full tumbler which had been placed on the altar during the operation.

The walls were filled in with old brick so that finally it was impossible to distinguish the old work from the new.

Mrs. Elizabeth Mosby, the first housekeeper, nurse and matron, is one more personality who was closely associated with the growth of the very young School from the time of its transferral to the Main Building. Mr. Joe says, "Her dominating personality, untiring energy, deep religious convictions and ability to grasp and meet a situation were absolutely necessary to get the School properly started. Mrs. Mosby was a large and handsome woman, a brunette already graying, when she came to Woodberry Forest. For the two years from her advent in February 1899 until Carter's marriage in December 1900, hers, not excepting the Headmaster's, was the 'strong hand at the wheel'. Her motherly affection for Carter, whom she always termed 'just a boy' (he was then 25), was to be a cherished memory throughout his life."

When the engagement of her favorite to Miss Hurt was announced, the first thought in the housekeeping department was, "Where are they going to live?" "In the infirmary and communicating bedroom, of course," said Mrs. Mosby. "But, Miss Lizzie," said Mr. Joe, "that is your bedroom." "That is my business, also. Joe, you get busy and build a closet under the stairway in the upper front hall, with the entrance enclosed and opening into their living room." "But that will ruin the looks of the corridor." "I can't help that," returned Mrs. Mosby. "You built the house without closets. Don't blame me!"

Another endearing personality came to be associated with the School because of one of the most trying moments of these struggling years. He was Dr. Lewis Holladay and the emergency was pneumonia.

Sam Orr was so ill that the teacher in the rooms on the third floor front was moved out. Sam was put in the study and his nurse in the communicating bedroom. Sam's father, a doctor from Anderson, S. C., had come himself to take charge. Everything possible was being done, but the patient grew worse.

In desperation, Dr. Holladay, who had just opened an office in Orange, was called in. The young doctor examined the boy and said to the Headmaster.

"If something is not done, that boy won't live through the night." "But Dr. Holladay, we are doing all we can." "What you are doing is all wrong. If you want me to, I will take charge of the patient, but I must have no interference and you must act quickly. I will wait ten minutes while you decide."

Dr. Orr admitted that Sam was slipping fast and agreed to allow Dr. Holladay to take over. His directions were given quietly and rapidly: "Get six hot water bottles, throw up all

The Woodberry Forest Baseball team of 1916.
Back row: P. Knowles, W. C. Leak, Jr., M. R. Baker, Randolph Scott, W. M. Luckett, G. W. Mercer, H. G. Gaver (Coach, Master). Front row: J. L. McCall, J. L. Sullivan, L. Wrenn, E. M. Jones, T. H. Wharton, H. L. Dechert.

three windows. Carter, help me move the bed between the two windows. Get three heavy blankets, two to go over the patient—he must not get chilled—and one to keep off drafts." Dr. Orr burst into tears and left the room. It was bitterly cold.

"No one must be in the room with the patient except the nurse and me. Send our suppers up here and a snack for the middle of the night. Also send some good, strong broth and a means of keeping it hot. The patient must have frequent nourishment, forced if necessary, and another nurse in the morning."

It is said that the courageous doctor held the boy's head out of the window and was rewarded by the return of color to the

The Woodberry Forest football team of 1919 was coached by W. R. Warren, (who later coached the first University of Virginia team to beat Yale), and numbered among its players Coleman C. Walker who eventually became chairman of the Board of the School. Back row: D. V. Richardson, Jr., J. R. Fain (Ass't Coach, Master), F. A. Godchaux, Jr., H. P. Foster, W. G. Stephenson, A. H. Harris, Jr., A. G. Metcalfe, W. R. Warren (Coach Master). Bottom row: T. B. Wright, F. O. Harding, J. E. Unsworth, J. B. Cheesman, A. P. Cutchin, C. C. Walker, F. H. Thesmar.

death-like face as he breathed the necessary oxygen. At any rate, Mr. Orr is, fifty years later, one of the top men of the Duke Power Company in South Carolina, and Dr. Holladay became the school physician.

Miss Maria Byrd Harrison is another personality whose usefulness was born of these growing pains and whose loving service became another tradition added to the School's long list. She came in 1907 and was for twenty years Senior Matron Nurse. "Miss Birdie" was always interested in making things more attractive for the boys, and by her frugality, vigilance and ingenuity, saved the School many a dollar in making use of any kind of material which might be considered worthless by anyone less ingenious. When she resigned in order to fulfill a promise of long standing to live with a friend, Mr. Walker wrote her in part: "For a full score of years, you have served the School with a devotion and loyalty which no contract could prescribe and for which money could not pay. Not only have you won the lasting gratitude of the officers of the School, the warm affection of the masters and their families, but you have endeared yourself to hundreds of boys who have passed under your care."

After 1914, when Mr. Carter Walker became the head of the family as well as of the School, another group of important and significant personalities began weaving themselves into the fabric of which Woodberry Forest had already been fashioned.

A colorful thread among them was Dr. William Rice Warren, who coached football in 1906, combined doctoring and coaching from 1917-1919, commuted between Woodberry Forest School and the University of Virginia for five years and finally settled down at Woodberry Forest School in 1924 as resident physician, a post he held for the next twenty years. Coach of the first Virginia football team to beat Yale, "Doc" was more than remarkably endowed for his service to the School. He has been known to say and to prove it that he could tell by the way a boy fell on the football field whether he was hurt or not. And it is probably some kind of record that in the 25 years Dr. Warren was at Woodberry, the School never had a tragedy in the Infirmary. His unerring ability to judge how sick a youngster was, no matter how much of a gold brick or how much of a Spartan he was, is a part of his great diagnostic talent. During all of his Woodberry life, which he voluntarily closed by retiring to enter private practice in Orange in 1946, "Doc" had and gave as much fun and dispensed as much charm and good humor as any one person is capable of. He was a marvelous shot with either gun or golf club, a bridge player of tournament calibre and a natty dresser. When "Doc" retired, a colorful and graceful figure was removed from the campus.

But he was hardly more of the essence of Woodberry Forest than "Mrs. Doc," who was ever a unique filler-in. She took on every job for which there was no other available hand, including holding "Doc's" instruments while he performed minor operations on squirming Woodberry boys; substituting for the nurse on her days off; keeping the Library; reading to Mr. Turner when his failing sight cut him off from his books; making cakes for school boys in exchange for their cast-off clothing, which she sent to her missionary society; teaching Doc's second form history class while he went fishing with Mr. Walker; and with it all, was the best conversational company anyone could imagine, for she was equally at home with a homesick little boy, an ill-at-ease visiting fireman or one of her colored friends, with whom she could chat for hours in his own vernacular.

In 1916 came William Leland Lord from Kentucky to teach Mathematics and coach baseball. His thirty-seven-year career at Woodberry Forest embraced the period of the largest growth of the School and established him eventually as assistant headmaster and a valuable cog in the wheel. They still say at Woodberry that Mr. Lord could do more things well than any man on the staff. Not only that, but "Uncle Billy" had perhaps the happiest faculty of all for enjoying boy stuff. For 37 years, he put up with everything from Johnny Mercer's eternal foot patting and drumming over his head, to swallowing down his own queasiness when a wag introduced a goat into his classroom and Mr. Lord insisted that the creature remain as a kind of punishment-fitting-the-crime maneuver. This whimsical gentleman retired in 1953 still deploring the fact that boys have gotten too sophisticated to indulge in pure devilment. Mr. Lord's easy-going acceptance of this kind of playfulness was evidenced some years before his retirement when he was enjoying the cool of the very late evening, sitting with Mrs. Lord in their garden adjoining the boys' dormitory. Suddenly he realized that a tall, young man who, a few minutes before, had been bedded down for the night by the master-in-charge, was now sliding down a sheet attached to the radiator in his room. "What are you doing, Tom?" Mr. Lord pleasantly called up to the suspended form outside the window. "Trying to break your neck?" "Yes, sir," came the startled voice of the thwarted gentleman who rapidly began to pull himself back into his prison. Not the least of Mr. Lord's value to the school was Mrs. Lord, whose delicious sense of humor and indulgence toward human frailty have always earned her welcome in any gathering and in any emergency.

Some others who were to add to the fine academic and athletic life of the School during the formative years were Cameron Wilson (1912-1921), Robert W. Fetzer (1909-1912, 1919-1920), Leonard W. Dick (1923-), Norton C. Pritchett (1921-1927) and A. Colquitt Shackelford (1922-1952). The

Leonard Dick, athletic director, demonstrates a football play to a group of coaches in 1947. Back row (left to right) Blair C. Gammon, M. U. Pitt Jr., Charles Rich and Ernest Crone. Front row (left to right) Robert C. Barr, Joseph M. Mercer, Charles E. Bettis, Samuel B. McLaughlin.

contribution of these men to what Woodberry is now could not be evaluated even if there were space to do so in this narrative. After the mid-twenties came a large group of men who helped shape the School into its present proportions. Many of these are still doing the same. They include Robert L. Rogers (1927-), Harry T. Saxton, Allen Barnett, Joseph M. Mercer (all three 1928-), W. O. Stackhouse (1926-1944), Arthur Latham (1929-), and C. W. Chambers (1930-). After them came a few rank newcomers who have been at the School approximately twenty years each, including Samuel B. McLaughlin and Fillmore Norfleet, both of whom came in 1934, spent a few years in other work and then returned; Charles E. Bettis (1935-), and these who entered World War II and went into other work following demobilization: H. S. Covington, Parks Harrison, Jack Frost, Paul Wilkinson and Edmund P. Dandridge.

Additionally in the '20's and '30's came a number of other members of the staff who were to make themselves invaluable and devoted contributors to the cordial, homelike and unselfish atmosphere that has always been one of the most contagious elements in Woodberry's atmosphere. There was Miss Constance Johnson, who came to assist Miss Birdie Harrison and remained to succeed her as the matron and morale-builder of dozens of homesick little boys and fun-loving big ones; Mr. and Mrs. Gouvernor W. Marchant—Mr. Marchant with his endless willingness to help everybody, from the little boy who had forgotten to get his mail to the master's wife who failed to remember to renew her magazine subscription, and Mrs. Marchant, who was simply dedicated to making life beautiful with her flowers, her food and her smiles; Mr. and Mrs. Woodson Harrison—Mr. Harrison who knew more about creating and serving wonderful food than anyone possibly could, and Mrs. Harrison who enjoyed the gracious side of life as only a sweet Southern woman can; Miss Imogene Marston and Mrs. Virginia Snead who successively held the post of secretary to the Headmaster, but who meant so much to him that he always referred to each of them as "My Associate"; and meant so much to the personnel of the school, that boys and masters alike depended upon them to solve almost any conceivable problem – personal or professional. Just before Mr. Walker's retirement as Headmaster, Mrs. Snead became the School's first Registrar and, in Mr. Walker's words in another reference, has become "his lengthened shadow." And there was Miss Ruth Adkins, the ever slaving and accusing nurse; and Miss June Anderson, the School's incredibly accurate bookkeeper. There have been many others, of course, but in the memory of almost any Woodberry boy, each of these will have some special significance in connection with something he may tell his children about his days at the Forest School.

There are still a few others who must be named because they have been more than just employees of the organization. William E. White is still head carpenter after a tenure of three decades during which he has been night watchman, truck driver, farmer, house painter and general dispenser of kindliness and helpfulness. "Willie is the salt of the earth," said Mrs. Joe once in summing him up.

Miss Fanny Watson came to Woodberry in 1916 to hover over the John Walkers' baby, Marie, but when that office deserted her, "Nana" took over two generations of faculty children as they came on.

The large number of faithful colored friends of the boys and the School cannot be left out of this chronicle. Almost first of all there was Mammy Deanie Gentry who reared the Carter Walker children. Virginia Snyder, "Miss Jennie" even to the boys, retired in 1953 after spending her whole long life at Woodberry, much of it in the linen room. Elijah Hopkins was head waiter for many years. "Snow," whose right name was

Robert Walker (changed to "Lewis" by Captain Bob), good-naturedly fetched and carried for everybody at Woodberry for 25 years and enjoyed the joshing the boys gave him as much as they enjoyed the sport. In addition there were Jim Tooms, Wash Lucas, Daniel Williams, Charlie Jefferson, majestic Landonia Dorsey and many of her children, and more recently, Isaac Scott, a student of theology and a man of vast dignity and devotion to duty. A story all in his own right was

Champ Francis, who had so many tricks and stories that the boys of his time knew Woodberry as well through him as through their other associates. A bit of financial persuasion could get him to do his famous imitation of Mr. Carter Walker telling a boy he must get a haircut. His reference to the Headmaster was usually, "Dere goes Mr. Carter Walker stompin' de yearth wit' his haid in de elements." Champ bent over a newly arrived master's wife once and respectfully asked her name. "I am Mrs. Lord," she smiled. "Why, mis'," he replied, "I couldn't call no lady by her husband's name. I means your real name"; and she was forever afterward "Miss Georgie" to him.

Chapter IV

BUILDING WITHIN AND WITHOUT

THE SCHOOL which was growing under the homely and affectionate ministrations of its faculty and staff, was by no means handicapped by academic makeshifts. Mr. Carter Walker had, at 23, undertaken the headmastership with an enducational philosophy which was as clearly defined in his mind then as it was expressed nearly sixty years later. Nor did he ever, in the years between, swerve from his original ideas:

"I went to college," he said recently, "with a profound respect for thoroughness. I had been more than adequately prepared for college by the teaching I had had at home and in the small school which grew out of our early tutoring there. I therefore found myself with two ideals: the value of hard work, regardless of whether the subject matter was hard or easy; and an uncompromising attitude toward honor in work and play. I realized that we had only these ideals upon which to build the School. Integrity of work, in and out of the classroom, and good sportsmanship have been the aims and yardsticks of the School from the beginning. Hard work is the greatest moral tonic I know."

In the early years of his headmastership, he associated himself with the Southern Association of Colleges and Secondary Schools, a natural move by which to acquire the proper "testing apparatus," as he called it, for the work in his own school. This association also provided Mr. Walker with some part of the education of himself as the pilot of the course which the School's curriculum was to take. He served on the Southern Association's executive committee from 1908 until he became president of the organization in 1913-1914. In these offices, he was an inflammatory spokesman against silly theories and muddy procedures in education. In many ways, he held no respect for the work of the public schools, which became a prey to these notions, but he stoutly and articulately maintains a high respect for public school teachers. He especially quarrelled with the public schools because he believed they disregarded the therapeutic and remedial values of hard work, for which he has a reverence, and used lower standards than were commensurate with the possibilities in their classrooms. For instance, it is utterly ridiculous to him to teach "character building and social adjustment." "They are by-products of education," he claims, "not topics for classroom discussion."

Mr. Walker's amazing foresight in academic matters seems to have been inherent in him, for he adopted the College Board Examinations "as a check on what we were doing" shortly after they were put into national use. For many years, Woodberry Forest was the only place in Virginia, other than Richmond, where these examinations could be taken.

"Even then," he says, "examinations were my hobby and an abomination of the public schools. I was interested in any kind of test which should determine the quality of work we were doing." It was that constant and tireless testing which was, early in its career, to earn for the School's production an enviable reputation in the offices of college deans of admission throughout the country. One of them wrote in recent years that "The Walkers have made of Woodberry Forest one of the great schools in the country."

It was, then, the teaching, which was being tested at Woodberry Forest from the beginning, and nothing better proves its superior craftsmanship than the fact that before the School was fifty years old, it had sent eight Rhodes Scholars to Oxford, a record surpassed by only four other schools (all far larger than Woodberry) in the country at that time.

Mr. Walker was a teacher of teachers, as well as of boys. He will disclaim much of the credit for this phase of his administration, but it is an inescapable conclusion that superior teaching, frequently by men with little or no other school experience, was responsible for Woodberry Forest boys' accomplishment in college. Mr. Walker was a constant student of his boys' school and college records, and through this study, he found out what was being done day by day in his own classrooms.

"I had frequent talks with masters, and also frequently disagreed with many of the best men I ever had about their methods," he now recalls. "I also had frequent talks with boys about their work and had great respect for their estimation of their masters." It is a tribute to Mr. Walker that a boy never realized he was being discreetly prodded for information about a teacher. Mr. Walker was adroit enough to extract this information from a student without his being aware of it. Through the years, Mr. Walker repeatedly whittled down masters as well as boys with blistering criticisms or admonitions, but it was always done privately. Many a teacher received a private rebuke behind the closed doors of the Headmaster's office after his position had been upheld to a student.

Mr. Walker had the happy faculty of never allowing a good job to go unnoticed, and in the hearts of most of his associates, the Headmaster's cordial thanks and expression of his good opinion were compensation enough. Moreover, there was not a one of these who did not know that the Headmaster was always on the lookout for him financially if he held up his end. After the transfer of the School to the Alumni with the authority vested in its Board of Trustees, Mr. Walker needled the board continuously for better salaries for his teachers, knowing that his own high standards could be upheld in the classroom only by first rate teaching, for which adequate compensation had to be made.

At the same time that the academic department was maturing, so was the Honor System, which is the actual government of Woodberry Forest School. Mr. Walker says that the Honor System originally was based on "Father's ideas of handling boys in the little home school." Many of its features were added by the Headmaster and based on the principles of the Honor System at the University of Virginia. Mr. Walker himself inaugurated the prefect system, which is the bulwark of the Honor System at Woodberry Forest. In his own words, he realized the necessity of a more complete cooperation between boys and masters at the time of the removal of the school into the Main Building.

"I called into my office a little boy named Carter Dillard, regarded by some as the worst little rapscallion you ever saw. I had lived in the room beneath his brother Dalton at the

The First Prefect Board.
Top row:
Edmund P. Dandridge, '01 (first senior prefect);
A. Dudley Carpenter '99;
Robert S. Walker '99.
Bottom row:
J. Edmund Price, '00;
William H. White Jr. '00;
Carter L. Dillard '01 (first prefect).

University, and I knew a whole lot about that attractive rascal, who later taught a year or two at Woodberry Forest. His young brother was a lot like him. I asked young Carter Dillard if he would be the first boy to undertake to put into practice this idea of mine to effect a closer working cooperation between boys and masters. I told him that I would ask four or five others, but that I wanted one first acceptance before I went further.

"He thought a minute and then said simply, 'Yes, Mr. Walker, I'll try it.' And that was the beginning."

The Honor System has undergone many reinterpretations and been broadly tested in the years since its inauguration in 1899, but its simple and straightforward original design has never been fundamentally altered.

As time went on and the Honor System became, under the Headmaster's careful administration of it, more integrated into the School technique, he became aware that the Honor System has two limitations: "It has no remedial procedure and it, theoretically at least, judges in the same way both the young and the experienced student." With this in mind, he spent many years trying to rewrite the statements of the Honor System in a manner better suited to the needs of Woodberry Forest students. In this work, he remembers he had valuable assistance from several of his senior prefects, notably Harriss Covington and Bob Lassiter. At long length, Mr. Walker says, he modified his administration of the Honor System, frequently being guided by information about infringements which happened to come to him confidentially. Naturally, when an honor case was picked up by the prefects, the Headmaster was always forced to handle it officially. He has always said, however, that he used to tell the prefects that although he held their judgment in the highest esteem and usually abided by it, the final decision had to be his own by reason of his responsibility to the School and the students.

It was with this attitude that Mr. Walker was constantly seeking re-examination of the work which his School was doing in order that its chief purpose—to prepare boys for college in every way—should be served in the most exact fashion.

Nothing better illustrates the durability of this preparation than a story told by a Princeton alumnus who was impressed by its impact. This Princeton man was at a party with the coach of a well known eastern university which regularly plays Princeton. The Princetonian inquired of the coach what sort of football team he was going to have in the fall, and the coach replied that he expected to have a good one to take on Princeton. At that, the Princeton man inquired about the eligibility of one of the players, a Woodberry boy, who was a fine tackle and was known to have been ineligible the previous season by reason of poor scholastic standing. The coach explained the player's situation thus:

"The trouble is that he simply will not crib on his exams. He sees other boys doing it, but he won't do it himself. You see, he went to Woodberry Forest where they have the honor system. Of course, it is a crazy idea, but after all, you cannot help but admire the boy."

While its inner man was being fed, the School was bursting, physically, at the seams. Even after the Walker building had been extended by wings added severally in 1904, 1905 and 1910, and other space for boys and masters added in 1907 by the erection of the small brick cottage behind the main building, a constant need for more space was everywhere manifesting itself.

One of the first urgencies during the very early building period was for athletic fields. One tennis court near the lawn and one combination baseball and football field (across from the present Hanes Field) were entirely inadequate. At a meeting of the School staff, the discussion developed two facts: some level playgrounds near the School buildings were a ne-

The Woodberry Forest championship football team of 1921. Joseph M. Mercer, who became captain of football in his sixth form year and later headmaster of the School, played end on this team. Back row: D. P. Douglas (Ass't Coach, Master), G. B. Taylor (Ass't Coach, Master), F. Mountcastle, R. R. Braswell, J. F. McGavock, E. G. Frye, H. P. Sanborn (Coach, Master), H. R. Labouisse (Mgr.). Front row: J. M. Mercer, J. F. Woodward, C. W. Gold, Jr., W. A. Devin, Jr., (Capt.) N. B. Barkley, J. W. Thompson, R. W. McClanahan.

cessity; and how to locate them on the ridge extending from "The Residence" to the Main Building was a poser. Clinton M. Kilby, master of mathematics, as well as coach, had drawn up a plan for a football field, surrounded by a track, and for two more tennis courts. Captain Bob asked for the plan, but had little to say about it at the meeting.

Before twenty-four hours had passed, however, Captain Bob was out on the hill northwest of the Main Building with Dick Marsh, his head carpenter. He was setting out stakes and showing Mr. Kilby what he had in mind. Hopeless as it seemed, Captain Bob was not dismayed.

"It will not be the difficult job I first thought," he said. "A cut of from three to five feet on the upper side of the ridge will level the lower side. I can make a good retaining wall on the lower side with hundreds of loads of rocks I've been hauling off the farm for years. However, I never thought I'd have any use for them."

Within days, the wall was in construction. It was fall then and the days were short, but Captain Bob and his men were at work as soon and as long as there was light enough to see. Farm teams were brought in to pull the plows and scoops, and by mid-March, there was a beautiful level, green field. The tennis courts were ready for the earliest spring tennis players.

A pool room in Orange failed and the properties were sold at auction. The School bought two good pool tables, built a small house for them south of the new field, and thus provided, without much trouble or expense, an opportunity for good wintertime amusement for both boys and masters. Later, when the space was needed for another playing field next to the Alumni gymnasium, this little house was moved across the road to a spot behind Anderson Hall and made into a dwelling for cooks and waiters, for which it still serves.

In 1923, with the enrollment at 165, the Board of Regents came to the conclusion that enlargement of the housing facilities of the School was now a pressing need and demanded solution on a large-scale basis. For this purpose, it appointed a Special Committee on School Expansion. This committee was composed of Carter, Joe and John Walker. A special meeting of the whole board and of the stockholders was called to empower this committee and its work. Three recommendations were adopted at this meeting: 1. That the necessary building be done (estimated cost, $100,000.00); 2. That the charter of the corporation be amended to permit the issuance of $75,000 of preferred stock to help pay for the improvements; and 3. That Frank S. Walker, president of the corporation, be the executive head of the building program. There is still extant a motion, written in Mr. Walker's handwriting, giving Mr. Frank full power to act for the corporation and to call upon the resources and assistance of any other member of the board to further the building program.

The project was eminently successful from every viewpoint. Up to that time, each boy in the four dormitories slept in a small "cubicle" furnished with a single bed, a bureau and a chair. He studied in another part of the building in a small room which he shared with one, sometimes two, other boys. This arrangement had not proved wholly desirable. By converting all the space occupied by cubicles and study rooms into proper living and sleeping rooms, some double and some single, an ideal solution to the problem could be met: the undesirable situation could be eliminated and more boys could be accommodated with better facilities for everyone. The program also included building a new cottage which should provide a dwelling for a master and his family besides living quarters for about twenty boys; for an enlargement of the dining room and the public hall; and for the installation of a two-pipe, instead of the old one-pipe, heating system.

To accomplish this extensive undertaking in the short time allotted, namely, from spring through the summer, without interfering with the School's program and in time for its September opening, required the ingenuity and ceaseless labor with which the enterprising Mr. Frank approached and accomplished it.

Mr. Frank had been made president of the corporation in 1921. His sound business judgment, keen understanding of building processes and intense devotion to the whole Woodberry enterprise were the constituents of the ideal director of this venture. His brothers cleared a path for him by providing every resource, even to keeping the workmen at their posts by night as well as by day. In the years that followed, he has continued this devotion to the School despite his preoccupation with his own interests. These include his farms, his presi-

Anderson Hall, Cottage B and Cottage A
(from left to right)

dency of the Maryland-Virginia Milk Producers Association, the chairmanship of the board of directors of the National Bank of Orange, and the presidency of the Orange-Madison Cooperative. Whenever Mr. Joe, the business manager, was ill or away, Mr. Frank stepped in and took over his duties. Since Mr. Joe's retirement, he has filled many a breach and maintained his vigilance over the entire plant.

The cottage built at this time was financed partially by Mr. and Mrs. Taylor, whose home it became, with the understanding that upon their retirement, their financial share in the building should be returned to them. Before two years had passed, Mr. and Mrs. John Walker had started another cottage next to that of the Taylors and under the same arrangements with the School. About this time, "The Cage," built in 1918, just at the east side of the Walker Building, was enlarged to provide a 50-yard running track as well as other facilities for wintertime indoor athletics, for which it still serves.

Shortly after these projects had been completed, it was realized that the Library had outgrown its quarters in a former classroom on the second floor of the Walker Building. Mrs. Joe devised the plan to enclose the porch in the angle between the front hall and the dining room, extend it upwards through the second story, thereby enlarging the library and providing the masters with a common room, which soon became a necessary addition to the dining room.

Beginning with 1930, the School building program made a new spurt and for all the work of that decade, the bricks in the lovely Georgian buildings were fired on the original kiln. Anderson Hall was erected that year, the handsome classroom building named for George Wayne Anderson who was killed during the last few days before the Armistice of World War I was signed. Seven years later, Turner Hall, named for Mortimer Austin Turner, "Able Teacher, Loyal Friend, Christian Gentleman," was built to house the upper form dormitories and the science laboratories. The Alumni Gymnasium was

The tablet on Anderson Hall, named in honor of George Wayne Anderson of Richmond.

dedicated in 1939. An extension to the Infirmary Wing on the southeast of the Walker Building was constructed in 1944. A residence for the business manager was built three years later. And with the acquisition in 1949 of "Brampton," the old Grinnan place adjoining Woodberry Forest, the extent of the school property was advanced to 985 acres.

Still another kind of growth manifested itself quite early in the School's life. It could be called "The Growth Upward." The early "Missionary Society" grew into the "Chapel Council," which now acts as the vestry of the Chapel and has made financially possible many recent physical improvements to the building, which has become increasingly more useful to the needs of the community.

In the winter of 1926, a significant event took place. Dr. Charles F. Myers, pastor of the First Presbyterian Church of Greensboro, N. C., whose two sons were students at Woodberry, came to the School for a series of services held morning and evening. Dr. Myers brought with him his church quartet whose singing was an inspiration to the entire community.

Prior to his coming, some of the boys had suggested that prayer meetings be held in preparation for his services. After he left, some of the boys said, "Why not keep up the prayer meetings?" And so was inaugurated one of the most distinctive traditions of Woodberry Forest, continued without interruption ever since. One evening every week during the school session, there is a prayer service which is voluntary, well attended, and conducted entirely by the boys with the oversight of their Chapel Council.

In 1932 a pipe organ was put in the Chapel which has added much to the beauty and inspiration of the services. The organ was provided under the sponsorship of the school paper, "The Woodberry Oracle," whose editor-in-chief, Aydlette Minor, solicited funds from many friends of the School.

Chapter V

THE SCHOOL COMES OF AGE

When Captain Walker died in 1914, he left the School, farm, and laundry property to his three eldest sons with three provisions: 1. Miss Nannie was to have her home in "The Residence" for her lifetime and also $20,000.; 2. the three younger sons Robert Jr., Frank and Stuart, were to receive $10,000. each; 3. the School debt of $90,114.36 was to be paid by its three legatees, Carter, Joe and John.

It was obvious that the small income of the School would not allow the three older brothers to pay these legacies and to operate the School as a partnership, assuming the outstanding indebtedness they inherited. It was therefore agreed among the members of the family to incorporate the business, issuing to each of the Walkers stock in the corporation for the amounts of their respective interests in the estate.

The first incorporation of the business was known as Woodberry Forest School, Incorporated, and was chartered as a private business corporation by the Corporation Commission of Virginia, May 12, 1914. The original incorporators and members of the first board (termed the Board of Regents) were: J. Carter Walker, president; John Scott Walker, vice-president; Joseph G. Walker, treasurer; M. A. Turner, secretary; Frank S. Walker; William Minor Lile, dean of the law school at the University of Virginia; Judge George S. Shackelford, Orange; Gardner L. Boothe, Alexandria; and A. Stuart Robertson, Staunton. Mr. Robertson was chosen by virtue of his having been one of only two boys who had twice held the post of senior prefect. It was felt that his youth and close association with student affairs made him a valuable addition to this body. Of the last four, he is the only one who is still a member of the School's board, having been for many years its secretary and a member of its executive committee. His home is now in Orange.

When the School opened in September 1914, the enrollment was ninety-six. Stock in the corporation in the amount of $172,000. had been issued, and the assets of the corporation (detailed by Mr. Turner in the original minute book) consisting of the buildings, farm roads, athletic fields, farm and school equipment and "good will" ($23,534.21), were carried on the books at $262,114.36. Twelve years later when the school was turned over to its present non-stock corporation, the assets, without any allowance for "good will," had grown to $709,370.45! This was made possible (1) by the sale of $75,000.00 of preferred stock in 1923, (2) by plowing back into new buildings and equipment all of the profits over a very modest dividend and the annual reserve for depreciation, and (3) by writing up the value of the buildings as the result of an appraisal made in 1925 for the purpose of determining the amount of fire insurance which should be carried on the buildings.

In a supreme effort to pay off the debt and continue building the School in every way, the Walker men and their plucky, uncomplaining wives, "put their shoulders to the wheel," as Captain Bob used to express it. In fact, it has always been an old Woodberry custom to double in brass. Everybody and everything through the history of the School has usually had more than one function. Extra compensation for this kind of thing was never a primary consideration, nor was it always forthcoming. As each new faculty wife appeared, the first thought was always where she could fit into this scheme. Her husband's job was seldom the only one in the family, and the Walker women set glowing examples of this system.

The undefeated football team of 1927. Front row: (l. to r.) T. W. Alexander Jr., D. A. Thompson, J. H. Lassiter, T. L. Parsons Jr., J. L. Peyton (capt.), J. W. Beury, C. C. Donovan, T. Rose, E. F. Clay. Back row: L. W. Dick (coach), B. W. Snyder, T. Follin, J. R. Weaver, R. H. Chatham Jr., R. K. Ivey, R. Lassiter, R. A. Tessier, S. W. Bodman, F. Dunn, J. H. McConnell (ass't coach).

Between the two world wars came the depression which colored and curtailed the technique of living at Woodberry Forest as it did everywhere else. It had its retrenching effects on teachers' salaries, enrollment and building, although it never slowed up the top-flight academic production to which Mr. Walker tenaciously held, using his original ideal of hard work and integrity of technique as grippers.

A different kind of coloring and curtailing of Woodberry life was effected by the two wars, to which the School gave the lives of fifty-four of its boys—eleven to the first and forty-three to the second. It is interesting to observe that at Woodberry, always dedicated to preparing its boys for their destiny and service to their fellow men, the emphasis on this preparation was wholly different during the two emergencies.

When the United States declared War on Germany in 1917, three students, Jack Hillyer, Duke Williams and Peter Knowles, and one master, George Wayne Anderson (who was

Woodberry Forest went military during World War I.

also an alumnus) left the school to enlist. Almost immediately, it was decided to put Woodberry Forest on a military basis.

Captain W. S. Noell and Frank Walker took charge of the drilling. They were succeeded by Major Charles R. Alexander of the Canadian Highlanders and a master of military tactics. Although he had been wounded several times in France and limped badly, he was a live wire and soon put "pep" into the daily drills. His Highland dress was picturesque and so was his language, for he knew all the swear words and did not hesitate to use them. No remonstrance from the Headmaster was effective for more than a few minutes at a time. Because of this propensity, he was dropped at Christmas and was replaced by a civilian who had had some military experience but lacked the hard-boiled spirit of the Canadian soldier. The boys took advantage of this deficiency, and one afternoon amused themselves by piling all the trunks on the corridor in front of his door. There was no drill that day—except that demanded by an irate Mr. Taylor who stood his ground with the culprits until every trunk had been removed and replaced in front of its owner's door.

When World War II seemed imminent, Mr. Walker considered the possibility of establishing another such military unit. Many parents urged the idea upon his consideration and many Alumni offered their resources for its operations. However, after writing to a number of schools, as well as to General George C. Marshall, the Chief of Staff, whose two stepsons had been Woodberry boys, Mr. Walker's own judgment in the matter was confirmed. The School concentrated upon the mental, physical and moral education of the boy and left the military man to be trained by the armed services. There was added to the curriculum a number of courses designed to give the boys rudimentary training in aeronautics, geophysics and other similar subjects. Into the bargain, the School program was stepped up by a nine-weeks' summer school program, so that a number of boys close to graduation might secure their diplomas before being drafted. War rations were strictly observed in all quarters, except that the school had a generous supply of meat from its own farm.

During both emergencies, Woodberry boys gave their energetic cooperation and by their own talents made a sizeable amount of money to give to the Red Cross. A Glee Club entertainment in 1918, given at the School in Orange, yielded nearly $100., but that accomplishment was practically smothered in effect by the auction sale which the boys dreamed up in

Henry Cumming, a graduate and later a member of the faculty of Woodberry Forest School, was the only Woodberry boy to represent his School on an Olympic team. He went from the University of Virginia to Amsterdam in 1928. He later lost his life while a member of the Armed Forces of this country in World War II.

the early days of World War II. St. Catherine's school in Richmond invited the boys to help them contribute to a canteen for the Red Cross. Instead, the boys decided to give their own canteen. They organized an auction in 1940, which was held in the Cage and offered at bargain prices everything they could beg from their friends and neighbors, all the way from a goat to the handsome furs given by a patriotic neighbor. Not only did the auction make enough money for a whole canteen, but the boys magnanimously made the St. Catherine's girls a present of an extra $100. toward their canteen.

As the years went on, the Walker brothers, each in his own way, gave much thought to the School and how permanently to insure its continuation as a Southern educational institution. They were rightly proud of the accomplishments of the School, which already in their thoughts had been dedicated as a monument to the memory and inspiration of Captain and Mrs. Walker. Eventually their hopes evolved into the ideal of taking the School from private ownership and placing it in the hands of an Alumni board of trustees so that the high purposes of the founder and the Headmaster might be preserved past any single lifetime or generation.

In a tentative move to determine how this could best be accomplished, an Alumni Committee on Reorganization was formed with William H. White, Jr. of Washington ('00) as chairman; Virginius R. Shackelford ('03), Orange, as secretary, and E. Addison Rennolds ('03), Richmond; James G. Hanes ('05), Winston-Salem; J. Lenoir Chambers ('10), Greensboro; and Isaac B. Granger ('13), Wilmington, N. C., as members.

Pertinent to the organization of this committee is an interesting meeting which took place in Washington between Mr. White and Mr. Joe during the period when these ideas of Alumni ownership were forming in the minds of the Walker family.

Mr. and Mrs. William H. White Jr. of Charlottesville who have given much beauty of all kinds to Woodberry Forest.

The meeting was accidental, and Mr. Joe tells about it through their conversation which he vividly remembers. As they encountered each other on the street, the men stopped for a greeting.

"Joe," said Mr. White, "I want to talk to you. I really wanted to see Carter but I guess you'll do."

"All right, Billy. What's on your mind? Come on down to the Union Station with me and we'll have lunch together. There is time before my train leaves."

"No, Joe, you come with me to the Racquet Club. We'll have lunch there. This is one time you're not going to be in a hurry."

Mr. Joe remembers the excellent lunch he had and how much he enjoyed it, as well as the pleasant talk, which obviously was not the business of the moment, despite the fact that he was getting more uneasy all the time because the time was rapidly approaching when the last train of the day left for Orange. Finally, over their coffee, Mr. White brought up the subject.

"Joe, some of us Alumni of Woodberry Forest want to do something besides just make a living; something for the South. We have decided that what is most needed is a good private boys' school like the great Eastern schools. We know that bricks and mortar don't make a school and that it takes years to build one even so. My idea is to make our own School that great school of the South. Some of the others think the Walkers would never listen to the idea of selling their School, but they told me to go ahead and try; that we have nothing to lose."

By this time, Mr. Joe was furtively wiping his eyes and hoping Mr. White would go on talking until he got hold of himself. Here it all was, being put into words and plans. Mr. White did keep on talking and Mr. Joe doesn't remember how he got back to Orange.

So the committee went to work on the following plan of reorganization: The Walker family, who owned practically all the common stock of Woodberry Forest School, Incorporated, except the qualifying shares of the other Directors, agreed that the then existing corporation should be changed to a new non-stock educational corporation not operated for private profit. All of the assets of the corporation had an appraised value at that time of $709,370.45. The new corporation would issue $300,000. of 6% 20-year bonds to be secured by deed of trust on the real estate with the understanding: (1) that the Alumni would sell for cash $120,000. of these bonds, the proceeds to be used to retire the preferred stock, $75,000.; to pay the mortgage indebtedness, $30,000., leaving a floating debt of $55,000.; and to complete the John Walker cottage,

$15,000., and (2) that the remaining $180,000. was to be delivered to the common stockholders for their shares of stock having a par value of that amount. In its final analysis, this meant that the Walker family, in furtherance of their desire to provide for the School's future, offered to give to the cause of education their equity amounting to $354,370.45. It was an amazing proposal, but no more so than their accomplishment. About twenty-five years before this, they had hardly more than Woodberry Forest, a $40,000. mortgage and their own industry.

While the preferred stock was redeemable at $105. per share, the Walker family, who owned approximately three-fourths of the preferred stock, declined to accept more than $100. per share, when their stock was redeemed.

The committee immediately undertook the task of disposing of bonds to Alumni and friends of the School, and succeeded in selling a sufficient amount to insure the completion of the reorganization. Among the first fruits of this measure in the reorganization was a remarkable gift by a number of

Mr. and Mrs. Walker and James G. Hanes at an alumni dinner in Winston-Salem in 1937.

these enthusiastic Alumni. Ten thousand dollars worth of these school bonds were severally returned to the school to establish the Alumni Scholarship Fund by the following men: James G. Hanes, John W. Hanes, Robert M. Hanes, Thurmond Chatham, Charles E. Norfleet, Charles F. Thompson, and E. Addison Rennolds.

In order, therefore, to make the School "more surely permanent and useful," it was chartered under the laws of the State of Virginia, and the formal delivery of the deed turning the property over to the new corporation was made on December 31, 1926. The original self-perpetuating Board of Trustees was composed of William H. White, Jr., Chairman; Frank S. Walker, President; John S. Walker, Vice President; J. Carter Walker, Headmaster; M. A. Turner, Secretary; Joseph G. Walker, Treasurer; and William Minor Lile, Gardner L. Boothe, Virginius R. Shackelford, A. Stuart Robertson and Lewis C. Williams. At the next meeting of the board held on April 4, 1927, two additional Trustees, James G. Hanes and E. Addison Rennolds, were elected.

The question is often asked, "Who owns Woodberry Forest School?"

The legal title of all the School property is vested in Woodberry Forest School, which is a non-stock, educational corporation not operated for private profit. The purposes for which it was organized were to purchase all of the property of every kind of Woodberry Forest School, Incorporated, and "to maintain, manage, operate and conduct an institution of learning for the instruction and education of young men and boys; to acquire real estate and personal property by purchase, gift, devise or bequest; and generally do all things that are necessary and/or incident thereto, and to have and exercise all other powers conferred by law on such corporations generally without exception." The management and control of the corporation is vested in the Board of Trustees consisting at the present time of 23 Alumni of the school. In 1930 the charter was amended so as to provide that the president of the Alumni Association, during his two-year term of office and for four years thereafter, should be a member of the Board of Trustees. The Board of Trustees is self-perpetuating as to the other members, one-third of whom are elected each year for a term of three years. This Board elects all officers of the corporation and has final responsibility for the policies and well-being of the institution.

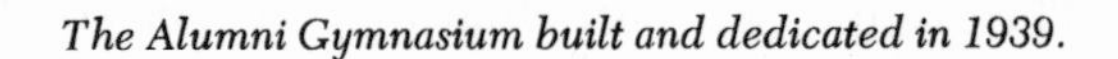

The Alumni Gymnasium built and dedicated in 1939.

Chapter VI

WOODBERRY FOREST AND ITS ALUMNI

SIGNIFICANT in the wording of the Reorganization prospectus sent to the Alumni in July 1926 is this part of the statement of the purpose of the proposal to take the School from private ownership: "It will bind the Alumni and friends of the School to it with stronger ties."

Nothing could have been more prophetic. A foreshadowing of this may be discovered in one of the old minute books. On January 1, 1925, the Executive Committee adopted the following project: "On recommendation of Mr. John S. Walker, he was authorized to employ Mrs. (R. W. D.) Taylor to help work up lists of Alumni."

Nearly six years later, in November 1930, the Woodberry Forest Alumni Association was organized with Harry Frazier as first president and Mrs. Taylor as executive secretary. "The incomparable Mrs. T.," as a retiring president of the Alumni Association recently termed her, has had a deep interest in her work and a devotion to it which can hardly be matched by any alumni officer in the country. In fact, many of them, from colleges and schools all over the United States, have sought her advice and instruction in her methods of keeping up with all former students. The number of the Alumni is approaching the 3000 mark and Mrs. Taylor, now assisted by Mr. Taylor in his retirement, is in touch with about 90 per cent of them. Whenever one of her "old boys" is to be married, the bell in the Chapel is rung by her own hands at the time of his wedding, and her wire of felicitations is in his hands by the time he leads his bride out of the church. The walls of her office are covered with pictures of Old Boys, beginning with photographs of the six little Walker brothers seated on the steps of "The Residence." One Old Boy is known to have said that nothing important had ever happened to him that did not bring an appropriate letter from Mrs. Taylor, reminding him that she was thinking of him. If her dedication to her boys can be summarized, the finale of one dear life might do it. When they found the body of one Woodberry Forest boy who had given his life on a World War II battlefield, it was discovered that the only letters on his person were Mrs. Taylor's last two, keeping him in touch with his old school. "Amici usque ad arras" are among the words of the School song all Woodberry boys love best.

That same auspicious day in November 1930 saw the dedication of Hanes Field, a gift of James G. and John Hanes of Winston-Salem, two devoted Alumni. It was the first big Alumni gift to the school after the Scholarship fund donation when the 1926 Reorganization plans were going through. The guests of honor on that day were two governors. Governor O. Max Gardner of North Carolina presented the field in the names of the two North Carolinians, and Governor John Garland Pollard of Virginia accepted it for the Virginia school. Almost incidental on this great occasion was the annual football game between Woodberry Forest and Episcopal High School. Governor Gardner's son, Ralph, was the fullback on the Woodberry team, and it seemed fitting that Woodberry should be the perfect host in every particular. "The High School" carried the ball over for the winning touchdown in the fourth quarter.

Hanes Field had been under construction for more than a year before its completion and dedication. Early in 1929 the Hanes brothers offered to give the School the best athletic field which could be designed, and Mr. Joe and Leonard Dick, the director of athletics, began their study of fields all over

Virginia and other states. Finding none that suited their specifications in every particular, they designed their own, crowned in the center, and having underground drains. Circling it is a cinder tract, bedded on crushed rock and bordered with concrete curbs. The cinders were procured by Mr. Joe in one of his ingenious maneuvers: after making the proper overtures, he secured a gift of two carloads of real cinders from the Chesapeake & Ohio Railway. An "anonymous donor" built the beautiful little brick field house, which stands beside the field.

Following this splendid token of the esteem in which the School was held by its Alumni, other buildings rose in time as further evidences of the affectionate concern of Woodberry's "Old Boys" for their School. In 1939 the magnificent Alumni Gymnasium was erected with substantial alumni help; and Woodberry Forest at that time was perhaps the best equipped preparatory school in the South. In 1948 the Alumni presented the Memorial Infirmary, a memorial to the Woodberry Forest boys who had lost their lives in World War II.

The practical and aesthetic manifestations of their devotion to the School's welfare by Woodberry's Alumni and patrons have taken many forms over the years. It is hard to put them into categories, because they usually assume, even in the eyes of the recipients and those who use and love them, a kind of personality which makes them seem as if they had all grown from the place rather than having been added to it.

For many reasons, it seems fitting to begin this register, incomplete though it must be, with those gifts which have emanated from the talents of Woodberry boys themselves.

About the time that the Alumni Gymnasium was in construction, Joseph M. Mercer, who was at that time the School's master in Spanish, was indulging his great talent for sculpture by modeling a large plaque showing heroic figures of athletes. When Mrs. Joe saw it, she was completely captivated by its value as an art object and immediately saw its possibilities as

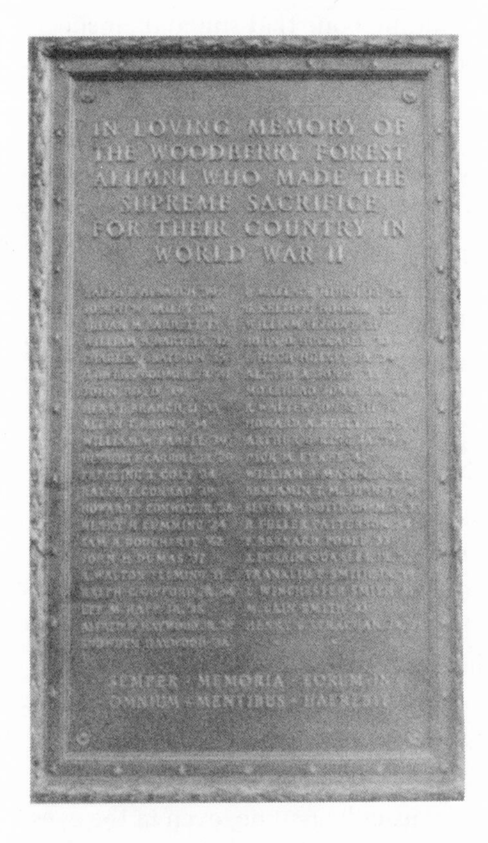

The tablet on the Memorial Infirmary, given by the Alumni to the memory of some of their old schoolmates.

a decoration for the new Gym. Learning that Mr. Mercer judged it too expensive to be cast in bronze, she brought the problem to the attention of an alumnus, Holland Judkins, who had it cast. It now hangs above the mantlepiece in the Memorial trophy room of the Gym, a fitting tribute to his old school from an alumnus-teacher who has become its Headmaster.

Joe Mercer was not the only Mercer to give a bit of himself to the school in which he had grown up. His cousin Johnny Mercer, the popular songwriter, composed a rousing football song called "The Orange and Black," which is a cheerleader's dream. Richard Preyer, who won a national schoolboy art contest while he was a student at Woodberry, has contributed a number of his paintings which may be seen in the Walker Building.

Among the many gifts made to his old School by William H. White, Jr., the outstanding one was his own personal service as Chairman of its Board of Trustees for nearly a quarter of a century. His unselfish and untiring assistance to two Headmasters and to the promotion of Alumni good will could never be estimated in either words or figures. Gifts to the School from both Mr. and Mrs. White have covered every

The Walker Building, 1954.

phase of the School's need and include their own books for the Library, as well as funds for the purchase of many others, the publication of a pamphlet including newspaper tributes to Mr. Walker on his retirement, many beautiful touches to the restored "Residence," an annually-awarded golf prize, and the stately new front porch and steps to the Walker Building.

Some years ago, Ben Finney decided to give the School a collection of wild animal heads which he had shot. His friend, Randolph Scott, the movie star, had them mounted, and together they presented them to their Alma Mater. Braxton Valentine and other Alumni have made a Mosby collection of books about the general, and together with a bust of Captain Walker's commander in arms, they compose a valuable gift to the library. Mr. and Mrs. Valentine also gave to the restored William Madison "Residence" a copy of the Saint-Memin crayon portrait of the original owner. The portrait of Mr. Walker which hangs in the front hall of the Walker Building was painted by Leopold Seyffert, the father of an alumnus, and together with a copy of Louise Young's portrait of Mrs. Walker, was presented to the School following Mr. Walker's retirement by William Camp, Randolph Scott and a group of Alumni. Duncan Groner gave the School a small and handsome library of books on art. J. Barbour Rixey, whose son was an outstanding Woodberry tennis player, established the annually-awarded School tennis trophy. Everywhere throughout the buildings and grounds are tokens of this kind of Alumni loyalty and devotion. A complete list of them is impossible to make.

Of a somewhat different kind of memorial are the many which have been dedicated to the memory of Woodberry boys who gave their lives too soon to endow their school in a material way. Chief, perhaps, among these are the memorial medal and the drinking fountain on Hanes Field to the memory of the only boy who lost his life in an accident at the

School. William Haines of Cheltenham, Pa., was drowned in the Rapidan River on May 3, 1929. In William's memory, his mother gave the drinking fountain, and Graham Cameron, who was saved in the same boating accident which took the life of his schoolmate, established the medal, still awarded at Commencement, for the best essay on a scientific subject.

Many of the Commencement medals have been awarded under such auspices. The Archer Christian Memorial Medal, considered the outstanding honor a graduate can receive, was established by the family of a Richmond boy, who lost his life in a football game the year after he graduated from Woodberry Forest. The Vivian Slaughter Memorial Medal, the William Barton Mason Memorial Medal (designed by Mr. Mercer), and the Leland Hume Lord Memorial Medal are all awarded in memory of Woodberry Forest boys whose lives were given in service to their fellow men. The Robert Williams Memorial Medal was established in memory of the first physician to the School. Also awarded at Commencement is the Sam Dougherty Memorial Golf Prize, given by his parents in memory of still another Woodberry boy who lost his life in the service of his country.

Mrs. Arthur Jones has established the French prize in memory of her father, Mortimer A. Turner, head teacher of modern languages at the School for many years. Also in Mr. and Mrs. Turner's memory are the Chapel's beautiful alms basons, another gift of their daughter.

In the Chapel stands the beautiful altar (mentioned elsewhere in this narrative) which was the gift of Alfred Baker Bransford's mother. A third memorial of a mother to her Woodberry Forest son is the handsome Memorial Room in the Gymnasium, which was the gift of Mrs. George Zinn in memory of her son who lost his life in a plane accident. The Chapel also has three memorial windows erected by Woodberry boys, the Walkers themselves, in memory of Captain and Mrs.

Archer Christian

Fuller Patterson

The Memorial Infirmary, 1954.

Walker, of Mrs. Carter Walker and of Mrs. Joseph G. Walker. In memory of Mrs. John Walker is one of the communion vessels and a pulpit Bible presented by the Rev. Beverley Tucker White. Some of the altar hangings and the pews are the gifts of Pittman Springs, an alumnus, and his mother. Mrs. Russell Bargamin, who was Mr. Walker's secretary for many years, gave the two front hymn boards in memory of her father and Mr. Turner. The prayer books now in use are the gift of the mother and the father of Stanley D. and Robert P. Petter, two recent graduates. The Rev. Charles D. Kean, an alumnus, gave the Chapel its beautiful Altar Book. (In the appendix to this volume may be found a list of all the memorial plaques in the Chapel and on various buildings.)

A fourth mother's memorial is the reception room in the Memorial Infirmary, given in memory of John O. Huckabee. Several other memorial rooms have been established in the new infirmary building, and among them is that given by Mr. and Mrs. Dillon Winship in memory of Blanton Winship who was killed in an accident while he was on his Christmas vacation during his Second Form year at Woodberry Forest. The

Shaun Kelly Jr. succeeded Mr. Walker as headmaster in 1948. He resigned in 1952 to become headmaster of the Casady School in Oklahoma City. He is shown with Mrs. Kelly, the former Jeanne Millet.

Joseph M. Mercer of Savannah, succeeded Shaun Kelly as headmaster in 1952. He is shown in the garden of "The Residence" with Mrs. Mercer, the former Virginia Boxley of Orange, Virginia.

reception room's guest book was given in memory of Herman A. Benton by his mother and father. Some other furnishings and additions to the Infirmary were given in memory of Leland H. Lord by Mr. and Mrs. Walk Jones and by Chester Brewer, '43. Mr. and Mrs. Robinson gave the new tennis courts at Woodberry in memory of their son, Elbridge Robinson Jr., '45, another victim of a plane accident.

The scholarships and other financial gifts to the School bespeak Alumni loyalty in another form. Among them may be mentioned the Fuller Patterson scholarship, established by his mother, Mrs. Henry B. Handy, in memory of the first Woodberry boy who lost his life in World War II; the Ida Lee Rust scholarship, established by her son, S. Murray Rust, '97; the Marguerite Alden Walker scholarship, established by John S. Walker, '97; and the substantial trust fund established by William B. Shuford, '26.

Elsewhere in this volume may be found a list of the gifts to the school which were made by each graduating class. That one is perhaps the only portion of this record which is complete. Woodberry boys and their parents have made such generous manifestations of their devotion to the School, that a mere summary cannot possibly be complete.

His old school has a special place in the heart of every man, and Woodberry Forest is perhaps no more blessed with devoted sons than any other alma mater. A preparatory school is only a springboard to life and every boy who leaves one to take a man's place in the world usually has a college, sometimes an "outfit," often a fraternity over which to spread his loyalty as an alumnus. In view of these later interests which come to almost every alumnus of Woodberry Forest, it is a constant source of gratification to us who remain behind that the old boys are always coming back to Woodberry. They come back in all kinds of little ways: by a telegram which says "It's a boy! Put him down for the class of '70"; by an outstretched hand, the owner of which says, "Don't you remember me? This is my wife. We are on our honeymoon"; by a letter from a college freshman: "Thank you for all you did for me. I got advanced standing in two subjects when I matriculated"; by the influx of Alumni from everywhere on that day in November when, every other year, Woodberry plays "The High School" at home. On the most recent of these occasions, one widely-traveled, sophisticated alumnus surveyed the large and colorful football crowd assembled from many far and near places, and said thoughtfully to his neighbor, "You know, I always knew Woodberry had something, and I believe this is it." In a different way, it was said by a young alumnus who returned on an uneventful day to call on his young brother-in-law, who was a student. The alumnus had just been liberated from a Communist prison camp, where he had spent two years after his capture during the Korean War. "I am not sure just why I feel so at home at Woodberry," he said. "I graduated from college and I spent a long time in the air corps, but somehow, I feel that my Woodberry friends are the best I have."

Appendix I

SENIOR PREFECTS

1900-1901	Edmund Pendleton Dandridge
1901-1903	Alexander Stuart Robertson
1903-1904	John Wesley Carver
1904-1905	Frank Palmer Christian
1905-1906	George Hermann Lang
1906-1908	John Victor Grainger, Jr.
1908-1909	Clarence Douglas Duncan
1909-1910	Joseph Lenoir Chambers, Jr.
1910-1911	Addison Baker Duncan
1911-1912	Thomas Cover Barton
1912-1913	Samuel Quinton Collins, Jr.
1913-1914	Barton Myers, Jr.
1914-1915	David Ellis Brown
1915-1916	Harry Lee Dechert
1916-1917	Joseph Morris Carroll
1917-1918	Ben Thomas FitzHugh
1918-1919	James Pickett Leak, Jr.
1919-1920	Coleman Carter Walker
1920-1921	Cornelius Monroe Vanstory, Jr.
1921-1922	James Epps Brown, Jr.
1922-1923	George Goodloe Early
1923-1924	Fielding Lewis Williams
1924-1925	David Watson Taylor, Jr.
1925-1926	Charles Newton Baker
1926-1927	John Cummings Wylly
1927-1928	Donald Alexander Thompson
1928-1929	Archibald Kimbrough Davis
1929-1930	Robert Lassiter, Jr.
1930-1931	Frank Hawkins Kenan
1931-1932	Frederic Hanes Lassiter
1932-1933	George Samuel Clarke, Jr.

1933-1934	Henry Wade Barrow
1934-1935	Charles Mellon Lowe
1935-1936	Charles James Hine
1936-1937	Mosby Gooding Cardozo
1937-1938	Howard Payne Conway, Jr.
1938-1939	Harriss Covington
1939-1940	Ira Griffin, Jr.
1940-1941	Henry Marston Smith
1941-1942	Oscar Green, Jr.
1942-1943	William Keenan Stephenson
1943-1944	Blair Cochran Gammon
1944-1945	Paisley Boney III
1945-1946	Robert Daniel Sellers
1946-1947	John Borden Evans
1947-1948	William Vardell Williamson, Jr.
1948-1949	Charles Lewis Haywood III
1949-1950	Murphy Evans
1950-1951	Harold Gerry Brown
1951-1952	John Carlos Dew
1952-1953	Victor Shaw Evans, Jr.
1953-1954	Julian Sargeant Reynolds
1954-1955	James Douglas Wilson

Appendix II

SIXTH FORM GIFTS

1924	Sixth Form Bench in front of Walker Building
1925	Flag Pole
1926	Portrait of Capt. Robert Walker
1927	Posts in front of Chapel
1928	Portrait of Mrs. Robert Walker
1929	Sundial at side of Chapel
1930	Trophy case
1931	Landscape painting in coffee room
1932	Landscape painting in coffee room
1933	Memorial tablet to Douglas Neff, School Chaplain
1934	Gate Posts at Hanes Field
1935	Drinking fountain at side of Walker Building
1936	Electric Clock in Front Hall
1937	Two silver vases
1938	Benches at North Entrance of Walker Building
1939	Tablet in Assembly Hall Engraved with Boys' Prayer
1940	Electric score board in Gymnasium
1941	Bulletin Board by Post Office
1942	Inauguration of Student Waiters
1943	War Bond for Alumni Scholarship Fund
1944	Benches on porch of Gymnasium
1945	Lamp post on lawn
1946	Exhibit stand in Memorial Room of Gymnasium
1947	Bell below Gymnasium
1948	Brick walk in front of Turner Hall and Anderson Hall
1949	Brick walk across lawn
1950	Lamp post on lawn
1951	Brick steps facing rear of Gymnasium
1952	Post Office boxes
1953	Portrait of Shaun Kelly, Jr.
1954	Lamp post near Gymnasium

Appendix III

MEMORIAL TABLETS IN ST. ANDREW'S CHAPEL

Armistead Mason Lee '00

Charles Frith Spencer — Master 1908-1910

Charles Theodore Airy, Jr. '15

Douglas W. Neff — Chaplain 1927-1932

Howard Payne Conway, Jr. '37

Severn Marcellus Nottingham, Jr. '32

Arthur Godwin King, Jr. '39

Leland Hume Lord '36

WORLD WAR I • 1914-1918

George Wayne Anderson

Frank Palmer Christian

Thomas William Cumming

John Victor Grainger, Jr.

Edward Valentine Lightfoot

Daniel Ashby McIntosh

Donald Fairfax Ray

Vivian Slaughter

Lewis Wardlaw Smith

George Clark Squires

Lee Campbell Tait

Appendix IV

A TRIBUTE TO THE MASTERS WHO SERVED WITH ME FOR TWENTY YEARS OR LONGER

by J. Carter Walker

At the very beginning of my headmastership, in September, 1898, I was joined by Mr. M. A. Turner, my uncle by marriage, recently released from the consular service. As he had been a teacher in his earlier years, he brought with him an experience that I sorely lacked. He brought with him also an accuracy in scholarship such as I have never seen surpassed. It was from him that I learned to be accurate in my use of English, whether spoken or written, and it was on him that I leaned for guidance in emergencies for more than twenty years. He has long since gone to his reward, a rich reward I am sure, but the good he did lives after him.

In length of service among my associates, my brother John exceeded all others. I cannot contemplate John's character without a feeling of humility, as nearly perfect as it is vouchsafed for a character to be in this world. By his own example he sought to point the way to good living, and in his gentle and tireless way, he strove to persuade others to share his convictions, that the examples we set are the most potent influences we can exert to help boys build good characters.

I turned to John first for advice in the emergencies that beset the path of a headmaster. I often rebelled against the soft words and gentle actions he counseled, but never without knowing in the innermost recesses of my being that he was right and I was wrong.

I would not hurry him on my account, but I should be mightily pleased if I could feel assured of having brother John by the hand when I knock at St. Peter's door.

Next in duration of service comes Rawleigh Taylor. Rawleigh Taylor joined us at Woodberry Forest in September, 1909. For thirty-nine years he taught Latin, and he filled a place in the life of the School too large to be easily described. For years he was in charge of the discipline of the School with the title of Senior Master. But it was as Head Teacher of Latin that he won greatest fame both within and without the School. Of the long line of masters who have taught Latin at Woodberry Forest, including the Headmaster, Rawleigh Taylor is "the noblest Roman of them all".

Leland Lord became a master at Woodberry Forest in 1916. He quickly identified himself with the School. For thirty-seven years he served as teacher of Mathematics, most of the time as Head Teacher and, for the last two years of my administration and the four years of the administration of my successor, as Assistant Headmaster. On occasion he could easily step into a vacancy in the teaching of such widely different subjects as Latin and Physics. Deeply religious, he was soon accepted by the Headmaster and others as the leader of the religious life of the community, and in this ill-cultivated field, rendered his most valuable service. We may feel sure that this truly great schoolmaster will be greeted on the other side with the commendation: "Well done, good and faithful servant."

For only a few years short of thirty, Colquitt Shackelford taught Mathematics at Woodberry Forest. A Master of Arts of the University of Virginia, he was well equipped, and no Woodberry Forest master was ever more faithful than he in giving the School the best he had to give. His sympathy with boys in difficulty, and his patience in helping them were unlimited. Many years, more frequently than not, he taught one class more than the usual teacher load.

It was in 1924 that Leonard Dick arrived at Woodberry Forest as an athletic coach and part-time teacher of English. A few years later he became Athletic Director, a position he still holds. During the ensuing quarter of a century, he played a most important role in promoting the growing reputation of Woodberry Forest. Beneath his modest and unassuming manner lay a determined and forceful personality that has left its impress of high standards in sportsmanship on hundreds of boys. Leonard Dick's influence today among the Alumni is probably as strong as that of any other master.

Harry Saxton became teacher of Chemistry in September, 1928, and soon thereafter head teacher of Science. For many years the boys who had passed his course in Chemistry earned, on the average, higher grades on the College Board examinations than any other similar Woodberry Forest group.

The last of this remarkable twenty-year-or-longer group, Joseph M. Mercer, the present Headmaster, also began his mastership in 1928.

Joe Mercer arrived at Woodberry Forest in 1919, as a little second form boy from Savannah. Five years later he graduated with top honors in scholarship and the reputation of being the best athlete in the School. In 1928 he graduated from the University of Virginia with honors in Spanish, having taught for two years a University class in Spanish with so great success that he was offered a teaching position as one of the University teachers of this language. Instead, he returned to Woodberry Forest as teacher of Spanish and assistant in athletics. During his twenty years of service with me, no boy who had passed one of his courses in Spanish ever failed the corresponding College Board examination, and those were the years of formidable Board examinations, or ever, so far as I can recall, failed in his later study of Spanish in college to win credit for himself and for his School. In addition to carrying during these years the normal teaching load, Joe Mercer coached three athletic sports, supervised the publication of the Annual, and was the master on whom I leaned most heavily in the administration of the Honor System. To an assistant master so versatile and so willing to render any service asked of him, no headmaster would fail to be lastingly grateful.

* * *

I deplore the limitation that deprives me of the privilege of including among these tributes the names of other masters who have rendered distinguished service to the School we all love, notably Fillmore Norfleet, whose superior scholarship has added dignity and prestige to the faculty of Woodberry Forest, and Arthur Latham, whose warm personality and the generous hospitality of whose home have enriched the social life of the School.

Surrounded and supported by such a group of men, no Headmaster could fail; without their help I could not have succeeded.